THE OTHER SIDE OF THE JORDAN

D1206613

Excavated Section of Ezion-geber, as it appeared in 1938;
Gulf of Aqabah in the background.

(Courtesy Air Officer Commanding, Royal Air Force, Middle East).

THE OTHER SIDE OF THE JORDAN

BY

NELSON GLUECK

Published by the
AMERICAN SCHOOLS OF ORIENTAL RESEARCH
NEW HAVEN, CONNECTICUT
1940

Copyright, 1940
AMERICAN SCHOOLS OF ORIENTAL RESEARCH

LITHOPRINTED IN THE U. S. A.
BY LITHOPRINT, INC., NEW HAVEN. CONN.

DS
111
.G57

And these are the kings of the land whom the Beni Israel smote, and
whose land they took possession of,
on the other side of the Jordan, towards the rising of the sun.

Joshua 12, 1

EMORY AND HENRY LIBRARY

71378

TO

HELEN

AND

CHARLES JONATHAN

TABLE OF CONTENTS

LIST OF FIGURES

Frontispiece. Excavated Section of Ezion-geber, as it appeared in 1938; Gulf of Aqabah in the background.

xiii

PREFACE

This book represents an expansion of the lectures delivered in America from October to December 1939 on behalf of the American Schools of Oriental Research. It is an attempt to give in generally accessible form the results of archaeological activities conducted in recent years by the writer as the Director of the American School of Oriental Research, Jerusalem, while on leave of absence from the Hebrew Union College, Cincinnati. The material is presented without the framework of critical apparatus, but also without the sacrifice of scientific exactitude.

No extended bibliography is being added to this volume. The reader who would like to pursue the main subject matter dealt with, may be referred to the following:

Explorations in Eastern Palestine, Parts I, II, and III (Vols. XIV, XV, and XVIII-XIX of the *Annual of the American Schools of Oriental Research*).

Bulletin of the American Schools of Oriental Research, Nos. 63-69, 71, 72, 74, 75.

American Journal of Archaeology, Vol. XXXVII, pp. 381-386, and Pls. XXXIX-XLV; Vol. XLIII, pp. 381-387.

Antiquity, December, 1939, pp. 416-424.

Hebrew Union College Annual, Vol. XI, pp. 141-157.

Illustrated London News, August 21, 1937, pp. 298-300.

Journal of the American Oriental Society, No. 56, pp. 462-471.

Journal of the Palestine Oriental Society, Vol. XVI, pp. 9-16; Vol. XVIII, pp. 1-6.

Rhotert, *Transjordanien.*

Detailed studies of the Omayyad castles dealt with will be found in Butler, *Ancient Architecture in Syria;* Cresswell, *Early Muslim Architecture;* Jaussen and Savignac, *Les Chateaux Arabes;* Musil, *Arabia Deserta.*

It is a pleasure to express here thanks to Professor Clarence S. Fisher, under whose direction the Index was prepared, to the Board of Editors of the Publications of the American Schools of Oriental Research, and to Professor Millar Burrows and Dr. Robert M. Engberg for their labor in seeing this volume through the press.

Thanks are due also to the *American Journal of Archaeology, Asia Magazine,* and the Pilgrim Press, which have generously placed some of their cuts at our disposal.

NELSON GLUECK

American School of Oriental Research,
    Jerusalem, March 1, 1940.

ARCHAEOLOGICAL PERIODS

Paleolithic	before 10,000 B. C.
Mesolithic (Natufian)	about 10,000-4,500
Chalcolithic (Ghassulian)	about 4,500-3,000
Bronze Age	about 3,000-1,200
Iron Age	about 1,200-300
(Including Israelite-Edomite)	
Hellenistic	about 300-63
Roman	63 B. C.-323 A. D.
(Including Nabataean and Thamudic)	
Byzantine	323-636
Arabic	636-1517
(Including Omayyad 661-750, and	
Crusader 1096-1291)	
Turkish	1517-1918

Chapter I

WHAT IS BIBLICAL ARCHAEOLOGY?

To the unlettered Arab it appears to be more than passing peculiar to see a foreigner walking carefully up and down and around an antiquity site, photographing, making sketch plans, collecting potsherds, and asking all sorts of questions about sources of water supply, names of the entire locality, whereabouts and directions of all the roads and tracks, and identity of the tribes, without giving him to understand what it is all about. I have on occasion been assiduously collecting sherds on a *tell*, when suddenly an Arab has appeared so to speak out of the blue, and asked whether or not it is some precious metal I am looking for, and if perchance the *frenji*, i. e. the foreigner, possesses some magic whereby he can change the dull pottery to glittering gold. Whenever possible, therefore, the polite and sensible thing to do upon entering a certain area is to find out who the paramount chieftain of that particular district is, and where he is camping, and seek him out, and pay one's respects to him. After all, one does not wander about in a strange territory, carefully picking up fragments of pottery from all possible places, without first making oneself known to the inhabitants and allaying the suspicions which naturally arise with regard to strangers in little visited parts of the world.

The hospitality of the Arab is a virtue which reveals him at his best. With much ceremony the visitor is ushered into the guest tent, in which there seems always to be a group of men seated around a central hearth, among whose coals a pot of long-brewed, bitter black coffee flavored with cardamon seeds is simmering. Room is made for the guest, extra blankets placed on the ground for him to sit on, a camel-saddle shoved next to him to recline on. Salutations are exchanged, one's health and well-being graciously blessed, and soon one is given repeated cups of the exceedingly strong black coffee, of which, to be sure, there are only a few sips in each tiny cup. It is a wonderful stimulant when one is very tired, but I shall never be able to understand how the Arab can drink cup after cup of it all day long at times, smoking innumerable cigarettes of native tobacco in the meantime, and still survive.

Then tea is served, and Arab tea is a concoction all in its own right. A small kettle of water is set on the fire, filled about half full with sugar, and when that has been brought to a boil, a handful of tea leaves is thrown in.

1

The mixture is boiled once more, and then served in small glasses taken from a special portable case, and carefully rinsed out by the host. When one comes in from a trip, hot and tired, and is given a glass of this sweet tea, it serves both as a food and a refreshment. But after several glasses it begins to cloy.

Before long, the noon or evening mealtime has rolled around. A huge platter is brought in piled mountain high with rice, on top of which swimming in oceans of fat and oil are large chunks of goat or sheep meat. One rolls up one's sleeve, gathers around, together with all the others in the tent except the host, and falls to. Proper decorum necessitates grabbing a fist-full of rice, making a ball out of it, and then ramming it down one's throat and tossing a chunk of meat after it. Mine host watches attentively, and occasionally flips a tid-bit of liver or a choice fatty section of sheep's tail to the guest, who must eat it or pretend to do so. In addition to this main dish there is the splendid flat, round unleavened bread, and dishes of delicious sour goat milk.

During the festal ceremonies, conversation of course is going on all the time. I think the Arabs are among the finest, and certainly the longest winded conversationalists I have ever known. However, it is not too impolite for the guest, after one of these overwhelming meals, in the midst of a sentence, simply to stretch out on the ground and go to sleep, after belching sufficiently to indicate to the host that the food has been wonderful, and that one has eaten to the point of absolute satiety.

Sooner or later during the visit, the host brings the conversation around to asking what it is that brings you into this particular neighborhood. It is for that question that the guest has been waiting sometimes for hours. You explain your interest in the history of the country, in learning, for instance, who the great, great, great grandfather of the host was. You explain, furthermore, your desire to wander about in the areas over which your host has general jurisdiction, in order to examine as many of the antiquity sites as possible, and request your host to accompany you. The explanation may take a long time, but it is the shortest and the safest way of attaining the desired goal, namely the invitation to wander at will up and down the length and breadth of the land, with the assurance of whatever assistance may be necessary.

Once the chieftain has understood more or less what it is that you are about, and has signified his willingness, nay eagerness to have you undertake the work of archaeological exploration or of actual excavation, then the first, and in some ways the most difficult step forward has been taken. By

the grapevine intelligence, which spreads with amazing rapidity throughout the country and desert, it soon becomes known that the foreigner
So-and-So, accompanied by this or that Arab, is the guest of the paramount
Sheikh, and woe betide him who does the guest any harm. It is for this
reason that during years of archaeological exploration in Transjordan,
accompanied frequently by only one Arab, sleeping often wherever it happened to get dark, rolled up in a blanket or in a sleeping-bag, no harm has
ever threatened us. Far and wide we have roamed alone and unarmed and
unguarded except for the far-flung protection of Arab chieftains. If indeed
there has ever been any danger while knocking about in Transjordan to
which we have been subjected, it is that on more than one occasion we have
practically been killed—with kindness.

To participate in a feast once in a while is pleasant and certainly bearable
at the very least. However, while the spirit is willing, the flesh is weak, and
after a while it simply becomes physically impossible to partake of many
of these gargantuan repasts. The Arabs when alone eat most frugally, and
it is only when an honored guest appears or a marriage is celebrated or
some other special occasion occurs, that the fatted sheep is slaughtered.
Several years ago, with Ali Abu Ghosh, my faithful companion throughout
long seasons of archaeological exploration, and the donkey-boy leading the
pack animal with our camp equipment, I had reached a pleasant hilltop
near the end of the day and decided to make camp there. Looking up,
however, we saw several miles away an Arab encampment. Custom dic-
tated that we should visit the encampment and pay our respects to the
chieftain who presided over it. It had, however, been a particularly weary-
ing day, and the prospect of partaking of yet another feast, and talking
then into all hours of the night, was too much to bear. We made camp,
had a bite to eat with a cup of plain tea, crawled into our sleeping bags,
and were soon dead to the world. A few hours later, we were suddenly
awakened by rustling noises. Looking about, we saw that we were surrounded by a large and menacing circle of armed Arabs rapidly closing in on
us. A shout stopped them, and then it took a very long explanation to
satisfy them as to our identity. Not having visited their tents when we were
so near, they thought that we must be up to no good business, which they
proposed to forestall before it could be executed. Had we not had something to conceal, so ran their logic, we would have presented ourselves in
the normal and polite fashion, and made ourselves known, and given the
Arabs the pleasure of extending hospitality to us. We talked ourselves out
of the embarrassing situation, and finally were left to sleep out the rest of

the night after we had assured them that we would appear on the morrow and have breakfast with them. We did not tell them that another reason for our reluctance to spend the night in one of the tents was a sudden but determined disinclination to be bitten to pieces that night by hundreds of tiny little guests certain to be encountered there.

The Arabs can be of great help to the archaeological explorer through their amazing knowledge of the districts they live or wander about in. When once they understand what it is that you desire to see, they will lead you to every ruin and every heap of stones for kilometers round about. Many of these, most of them, may turn out to be of no importance whatsoever, but some of them are of the utmost significance. And again, one learns from contact with the Arabs, and from the traditional customs they still retain to a greater or lesser degree, much about the ancient past in which one is particularly interested. On one occasion, for instance, when we were being entertained by an important tribal chieftain in southern Transjordan, a feast was prepared in honor of our company which gave us pause to think not only because of its richness and size, but primarily because of the nature of the main dish. The *pièce de résistance* consisted of a young kid boiled in the milk of its mother. Shades of the Biblical prohibition, forbidding most expressly just that particular dish! " Thou shalt not boil a kid in the milk of its mother," the Bible commands. On the basis of that statement, Jews during the course of centuries have built up an entire ritual based on the distinction between meat and milk foods. In northern Syria, however, in the excavations at Ras Shamra, cuneiform tablets were found, one of which told that the most proper way to honor one of the pagan deities was to bring an offering of a young kid boiled in milk. The custom has been maintained to this very day. The guest, like the god, is to be honored with the famous delicacy. When the religious leaders of Israel sought to keep their people away from the pagan practices of the Canaanites, among which evidently was the one of offering this particular sacrifice to one of the fertility deities the Israelites were rapidly learning to worship in their new environment, the law was passed, in the attempt to wean the backsliders away from the pagan practices, " Thou shalt not boil a kid in the milk of its mother " (and bring it as an offering to one of the gods).

However, too much may not be expected by the student from habits and customs prevalent today in Bible lands. First of all, many of them may go back merely to Crusader or Byzantine times, and have absolutely nothing to do with the earlier Biblical periods or scenes. Much of ancient lore and habit that has been long preserved is dying out. The equivalent of the troubadour reciting epic tales, learned from his father, to awe-stricken groups, is being replaced by gramaphones or radios blaring raucous tunes. The advance of modern customs and dress and appliances appears to be irresistible throughout the Near East. Even in Transjordan, which has remained comparatively unaffected by the impact of modern civilization, when contrasted with Palestine, distinct changes from the old to the new can be observed. Autobuses and passenger automobiles in an ever increasing number take the place of caravans of camels. The tinkling of the camel-bell is rapidly being silenced. The heavily loaded, lightly treading, eternally chewing, supercilious looking camels, and the solemn, sad looking, wise little donkeys leading them are being pushed more and more into the background. The songs of their drivers and the sweet sounds of the flute are being heard much less than hitherto. Soon the day may pass altogether, except in outlying regions, when the angry driver can be seen spitting into the face of his obstinate donkey, and be heard yelling at it in a frenzy of profanity: " Cursed be thy religion." The empty, ugly gasoline tin is taking the place of the native, shapely, earthenware water-jug.

The peasants cling, however, to many of their old superstitions, howbeit in altered form. The invisible spirit whom they still fear must be appeased, even if it is an automobile and not a sheep or a horse that must be protected. Thus the amulets and beads and colored strings which graced the necks of the animals have now in large part been placed upon the radiator caps and steering wheels of the new four-wheeled, gasoline-consuming contraptions, about which new legends have sprung up. According to one account, there is a spirit or *djin* that sits underneath the hood of each automobile. He drinks the gasoline, in return for which he makes the wheels go round. When an accident occurs, the explanation is that the *djin* is angry. In other instances, we find ancient customs being arrayed in modern garments. On one occasion, we saw the evil spirit being driven out of sick sheep by rifles being fired over their heads. The sheep scampered away half scared to death. We did not wait to see how effective the cure was.

We stood bemused one day in front of an ancient ruin in South Gilead, belonging to the Early Iron Age. Its walls were built of huge blocks of stone, measuring about 1.20 by 1 by .80 meters. The local Arab guide had a ready explanation of how the ancients erected walls of such stones, which today would require heavy hoisting machinery. " Do you know, O Effendi, that generations back, this land was peopled by giants? For one of them to lift one of these huge blocks, is as if I were to lift up one of the small stones at my feet." Small wonder that to the simple scouts of the nomad Israelites

the Canaanite cities appeared to be " strong and fortified up to the heavens."
The very inhabitants of the land appeared like giants to them, " children of
Anaqim." [1]

II

Despite all the growth and change in manner and custom and culture
among the Arabs in Transjordan and particularly in Palestine today, there
is one group which shows essentially no change whatsoever throughout the
course of the centuries and the millennia. That group is composed of the
Bedouins, particularly those of them that tent and wander in the desert.
The economy of all of them to be sure has in some way or other been affected
by the impacts of modern life. The use of firearms and tobacco and sugar
and tea has penetrated into the innermost fastnesses of the desert. Essentially, however, the nomads of greater Arabia are but little different today
from their predecessors hundreds and thousands of years ago. Always they
are hungry, and unceasingly they cast longing eyes upon lands which to
them are lands flowing with milk and honey.

The struggle between the Desert and the Sown seems to be a perpetual
one. The moment that the central political authority weakens or is
destroyed, that moment the Bedouins sweep in, carrying all before them.
As late as 1921, a group of approximately 3000 Bedouins on camels raided
into Transjordan from Arabia, and were within three hours' striking distance of Amman, the capital, before a squadron of bombing planes and a
number of armored cars could be brought up, and effectively disperse them.
Like the waters of the ocean, the Bedouins may be held in check, but the
moment the barriers are weakened, in they sweep with a destructive force
that cannot be stemmed. At present, the eastern frontier of Transjordan
facing the desert is well guarded by a long line of frontier posts, surrounded
by barbed-wire entanglements, equipped with machine-guns, receiving and
sending radio sets, armored cars, landing fields, and cisterns filled with water.
By them may be seen the tents of the Bedouins who may not remember, but
who nevertheless instinctively must know, that others like themselves camped
in days gone beside similar Roman and earlier fortresses back down through
the annals of history; and that always the Bedouins have finally won out, as
each civilization in turn has either destroyed itself or been destroyed.

To judge from the ruins which the archaeologist visits, and the sherds of
all the historical periods of the past with which he plays, history will inexor-
ably repeat itself, and in some future day the descendants of the present

[1] Numbers 13, 28; Deuteronomy 1, 28, and 9, 2.

day Bedouins will be camping by the ruins of the modern Transjordanian frontier posts, with no one to stay their wanderings or control their movements. In all of the history of Transjordan, the single force which stands out at once as the weakest and the strongest, as the most fluid and the most lasting, is that of the indestructable Bedouins. They can always retreat into the desert whither few can follow, and they are always prepared to break into the fertile lands at the first appearance of weakness there. They can live on next to nothing, and have the patience of the ages. Of the Bedouins it may be said that it is the weak who shall inherit the fruits of the earth. It is only when the Bedouins seize the acres of the Sown, and become by the force of circumstances agriculturists in their own right, that they are subject to the forces of growth and decay, from which in their native state they are secure. There are, however, always enough of their original kind left behind them to enable the eternal struggle to continue, with the chances for final victory inevitably weighted in favor of the Bedouins.

III

Ancient sites are not discovered by divining rods, yet the archaeologist must always be on the lookout for water. In all lands, but particularly in such semi-arid countries as Western Palestine (Cisjordan) and Eastern Palestine (Transjordan), which in the Bible is known as the Other Side of the Jordan, the location of a settlement is determined by the presence of an adequate water supply. He who would rediscover there the sites of ancient villages and towns and fortresses must first of all find out where streams or springs or wells exist or once existed. It is natural that in such an environment pagan belief emphasized the importance of those deities who controlled the rains and regulated the flow of waters, and thus conditioned the fertility of the soil. Small wonder that water rights were the bases of quarrels,.and the discovery of new water a source of great joy. We read in Numbers 21, 16-18:

From there they proceeded to Beer (Well), which is the well where the Lord said to Moses: 'Collect the people, and I will give them water.' It was then that Israel sang this song:

> Spring up, O well! Sing to it.
> The well which the princes dug,
> Which the nobles of the people sunk,
> With scepters, with their staffs.

The Israelites on their way from Sinai through Transjordan to the Promised Land undertook to pay for whatever water they drank. With reason

Achsah asked for the upper and lower springs bounding the field her father had given her bridegroom, Othniel, as a marriage gift.

'Give me a blessing,' she said to her father: 'for thou hast given me a south land; give me also springs of water.' And Caleb gave her the upper springs and the lower springs.[2]

Thus, where there is a strong spring, a good well, or a perennial stream, one can almost always find traces of an early settlement.

IV

Other points also in the geography and topography of these Bible lands must be carefully considered. The ancient highways and side roads in Transjordan, for instance, follow the length of the fertile, high plateau backbone of the country, and the lines of the natural geographic divisions formed by the large and small stream-beds. Some of these stream-beds are dry, being flooded with water only during the rainy season. Others, such as the Wadi Hesa (the Biblical River Zered), the Wadi Mojib (the Biblical River Arnon), the Wadi Zerqa (the Biblical River Jabboq), and the Wadi Yarmuk carry perennial streams of water, which grow to the magnitude of rivers during the winter or rainy season. (The name for these stream beds in the singular in Arabic is *wadi,* and in the plural is *wudyan.*) (Fig. 1.)

Whole strings of settlements are commonly found overlooking particularly those *wudyan* in the bottoms of which continuous streams flow, and in other instances overlooking or situated at places along their slopes where springs emerge. On the Moabite stone, Mesha, the king of Moab who succeeded in restoring the independence of Moab at the end of the reign of Ahab, king of Israel, tells how he had a road and a number of towns built along the top of the north side of the River Arnon.

Close to the surface of some of these *wadi*-beds sub-surface water can be found. The ancients were even more familiar with this phenomenon than the modern Arabs of Transjordan, and a number of important ruins were found overlooking dry *wadi*-beds, which upon examination yielded copious water supplies after digging little more than half a meter below the surface. Khirbet Medeiyineh,[3] overlooking the Wadi Themed in Transjordan, must have depended for a large part of the year upon the subsoil water obtainable in the *wadi* by digging shallow holes, just exactly as the Bedouins of the

---

[2] Judges 1, 15.

[3] Detailed maps showing the location of Transjordanian sites may be seen in *Annual of the American Schools of Oriental Research*, Vol. XVIII-XIX (1939).

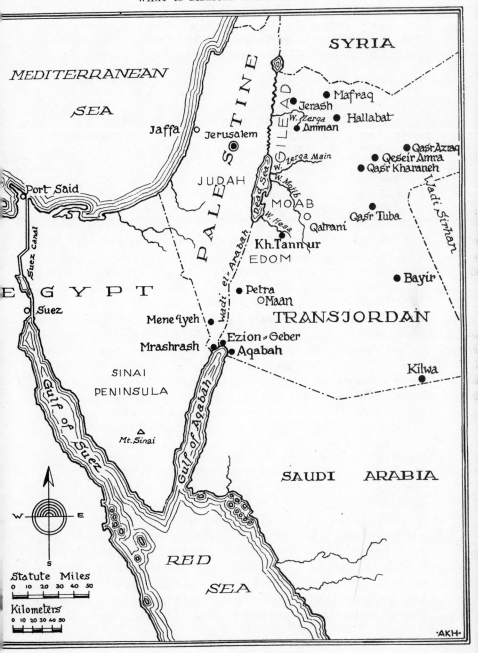

Fig. 1. Map of Transjordan.

district do to this very day. One recalls the Biblical description in II Kings 3, 16. 17 in which the phenomenon of water being produced from apparently dry *wadi*-beds is described in the language of religious experience:

Thus saith the Lord, 'I will make this torrent-bed nothing but cisterns. . . . You will see neither wind nor rain, yet the torrent-bed shall be filled with water.'

The Government of Transjordan is today constructing a main north-south vehicular highway, which bisects the long, fertile, comparatively well-watered part of the Transjordan plateau. This fertile strip is bounded on the west by the descent to the depression formed by the Jordan River Valley, the Dead Sea, and the Arabah rift, and on the east by the desert. The new roadway is complete now for almost its entire length from the border of Syria to the Gulf of Aqabah, the northern and southern limits of Transjordan. It is already in use from Kerak (the Biblical Qir-Hareseth) to Elji, the modern Arabic village at the entrance to Petra, and to Aqabah, the modern successor of Roman and Nabataean Aila and of King Solomon's earlier seaport, Ezion-geber. The stretch from the Syrian border to Amman and then to Madeba has also been travelled on for some time now. It is only from Madeba southward that the new road is incomplete, because the great canyon of the Wadi Mojib presents a difficult but far from insuperable problem in highway engineering. When the new road completes its zigzagging course, already commenced, down one side and up the other side of the Wadi Mojib, the entire project will be complete. The modern inhabitants of Transjordan will then be able to use a road throughout the length of the central and richest part of their country, which was traversed along almost exactly the same line in every period of the past, and which has been famous in the annals of the country from the earliest times of its recorded history.

The new roadway follows almost exactly the line of the famous Trajan highway, built in the very first part of the second century A. D. This ancient road stretches in a clearly traceable line all the way from Bosrah, just across the Syrian border, to Aqabah. For miles the modern highway parallels the Roman road; frequently it crisscrosses it, and for long stretches is built directly over it. At many places alongside of the modern roadway may be seen to this very day Roman milestones, marking the path of the earlier road. Indeed, the modern road engineers might have been instructed from the very start simply to follow the line of the old Roman road, had they had an archaeologist or two along to help point it out to them. They would have been spared much of the labor of surveying the new line, which for all practical purposes overlaps the Roman one. It is only when the line for the road down and up the sides of the major *wudyan*, such as the Wadi Mojib and the Wadi Hesa, had to be fixed, that the line surveyed by the modern engineers differs radically from the line of the Roman road. That

Fig. 2.   Roman Road east of Wadi La'ban.

(Courtesy Air Officer Commanding, Royal Air Force, Middle East).

line can still be seen clearly, especially from an airplane. Not having to consider automobile traffic, the Roman engineers could run their roads up and down the steep slopes of these great *wudyan* in a much more direct line than the modern engineers, who are compelled to choose a much more zigzag course. And that is about the only main difference between the two

roads, the one built near the beginning of our era, and the other in the
20th century A. D. (Figs. 2 and 3).

Other differences could be detailed, to be sure, but they would not cast a

Fig. 3. Roman Road on north slope of Wadi Mojib.

(Courtesy Air Officer Commanding, Royal Air Force, Middle East).

favorable light upon the methods of the modern road-builders in Transjordan. The Romans paved their highway all the way from its very beginning to its very end. It was divided into two lanes, with a protruding line
of stones in the middle, and the sides of the road also marked by raised
stones. I have seen large stretches of the modern road washed away after

the first rain. The Romans, however, were such excellent engineers that miles upon miles of their roadway still remain comparatively intact, and where sections are missing it is at least as much due to the ravages of man as to the ravages of time. I have flown over one side-branch of this remarkable road, which leads from Kerak down to the Lisan, the small peninsula that projects into the eastern side of the Dead Sea. From the air it looked like a modern highway, and I who prided myself on knowing all the roads in Transjordan, was astounded for a moment that this one had escaped my attention. I soon realized, however, that I was not looking at any modern road, but at a branch of the famous Trajan road. It traverses a part of Transjordan which today is little inhabited and infrequently travelled, and is still in an amazing condition of preservation (Fig. 4).

It is natural that along the Trajan highway there should be found many ruins that can be dated to the period of the Roman domination of the country. It soon becomes apparent, however, that the country's natural geographical and topographical features have conditioned in all periods of the past as they must in all periods of the future the places of settlement and the directions of the roads. The same line of travel which was used for the construction of an elaborate highway by the Romans, was used in large part before them, particularly in southern Transjordan, by the Nabataeans, whom the Romans finally conquered under Trajan in 106 A. D.

The Nabataean civilization, as we shall have occasion to enlarge upon later, was in many ways the finest of all those which rose and fell in Transjordan. Their caravans trafficked up and down the central highway, bringing the products of Arabia northward and carrying the goods of Syria southward. Their pottery has been found at Jerash, indicating that Nabataean trade extended beyond the confines of their territory in southern Transjordan. Nabataean pottery has also been found at Teleilat edh-Dhahab, near the western end of the Jabboq River before its descent into the Jordan River Valley, showing that Nabataean caravans may have followed this important side road which led westward to Palestine. Nabataean stations marked with thousands of fragments of Nabataean pottery have been found all along the length of the Wadi Arabah, and along the tortuous pass leading up the Neqb Sfar from Ain Hosb in the Wadi Arabah, and passing Qurnub to Gaza on the Mediterranean. From Gaza and Ascalon, vessels carried Nabataean merchandise to Rhodes and Italy and Alexandria and elsewhere along the Mediterranean. In southwestern Palestine and in southern Transjordan, very many, if not practically all of the Nabataean settlements were taken over by the Romans.

Fig. 4. Roman Road leading from Kathrabba to Dead Sea.
(Courtesy Air Officer Commanding, Royal Air Force, Middle East).

Once it has been possible for the archaeological explorer to ascertain the main lines of the highways in a country such as Transjordan, an important prerequisite of his work has been accomplished. Of course, in actual practice, the procedure does not work out with such elegant simplicity. Frequently he must work in the dark, and only after discovering many isolated settlements, and plotting them on a map, does it become manifest that they are following natural physical lines of a country. Where they do not, then there must be some particular economic or other understandable reason for their existence. In the Byzantine period, monks built cells in the most out of the way places, in order in undisturbed solitude to seek communion with the divine.

The main central highway throughout the length of Transjordan was old even before the Nabataeans appeared upon the scene. Centuries and millennia before them, the same line of roadway was already in use, because of practically the same geographical, topographical, and economic reasons. When the messengers of Moses came from Qadesh-Barnea to the kings of Edom and Moab, they promised them that the Israelites would hew to the line of the " King's Highway," the royal road, turning neither to the right nor to the left of it, and paying for whatsoever they obtained in food and drink. What is this " King's Highway " which cut through central Transjordan as early as the time of Moses? Where did this " royal road " lead to? As must already be apparent to the reader, it is nothing more and nothing less than the very same highway, or the line of that highway which in due course of time became Trajan's Road, and which today has become Emir Abdullah's road. It is called in the modern Arabic vernacular, *et-Tariq es-Sultani*, the Sultan's Road. The King's Highway led from Aqabah to Syria. Along its length, and marking its character as clearly as if there had been Roman milestones with Latin inscriptions or modern Transjordanian sign-posts with Arabic letters, have been found numerous sites, which can be dated by pottery finds between the 13th and 6th centuries B. C.

As a matter of fact, a thousand years before the time of the King's Highway the same line of roadway was used throughout Transjordan. Its entire length has now been traced by means of the ruins of large and small ancient sites which can be dated approximately between the 23rd and the 20th century B. C. The presence not only of a civilization, but particularly of a main highway in Transjordan in this period is already adumbrated in the pages of the Bible. In the 14th chapter of the Book of Genesis there is the account of the Eastern Kings who swept through the length of Transjordan,

3

all the way to El-paran, which may possibly be situated on the north shore of the Gulf of Aqabah. They evidently left destruction behind them. Whether or not they were part of the great Hyksos invasion is not known. It is clear from this account in Genesis, that the period in question may roughly be equated with the Age of Abraham. The archaeological finds show that many of the sites in Transjorden which belong to this period are exactly along the most likely route of march that the armies of the Eastern Kings would have taken, namely the line used in every subsequent period of history. The importance of the discovery of this long line of early Bronze Age settlements throughout the length of Transjordan lies first of all in the fact that their presence authenticates the general validity of the background of Genesis 14, and secondly that once again we are confronted with the main north-south travel-route.

It has thus far been possible to trace the history of this famous road from several centuries before the 20th century B. C. all the way down to the 20th century A. D., a span of more than 4000 years. It may be accepted as axiomatic, that from the very dawn of history in Transjordan this central track through the country was always the main line of march. And as long as the country retains its present physical features, and human beings remain to people it, this central track will continue to be used. There will remain to mark it, in centuries and millennia to come, vestiges also of still future civilizations that are destined to develop and disintegrate or be destroyed in it during the long march of time.

V

It behooves the archaeological explorer in such lands as Palestine and Transjordan not only to pay attention to the major geographical and topographical features of the country, but also to look carefully along the landscape for sites which could be easily fortified. The ancients indulged in a habit which is commonly practiced to a large degree in our own day. They used to fight with each other on all possible and impossible occasions. On the whole, however, they kept their struggles within comparatively civilized bounds. In the lands we are particularly interested in, the state organizations were not as cohesive and strong as those of the modern states, and each community was often put to it to fend for itself. A general rule, however, cannot be applied to all the civilizations that can be traced in the early history of Transjordan with regard to the inner strength or weakness of the various political entities that existed there at one time or another, with greater or less power to protect their corporate parts. To a great extent in the early part of the Bronze Age, less in the Early Iron Age, and to a still lesser extent in the subsequent Nabataean and Roman periods, each settlement was compelled to provide for its own protection. It was natural therefore, particularly during the earlier periods of settlement in Trans-jordan, for each community to select as a dwelling site a place situated not only by an adequate water supply, and on or near some highway, but also at a point which could be easily fortified, and which by its very position would lighten the task of defence measures.

The approaches up a fairly steep hillside could naturally be more easily defended against an enemy than if the paths led to a village on a plain. In addition, once the crown of a hill was covered with the houses of the first village erected there, the entire village could be surrounded by a strong fortification wall, adding to the strength of the position itself. Not infre-quently, to make insurance doubly sure, so to speak, the inhabitants of a fortified village or town situated on top of a hill or even of some small rise or eminence, would dig a deep and, if need be, long tunnel from inside the village through the entire depth of the hill until some subterranean supply of water was tapped. The villagers would then be assured of a constant supply of water, even if the enemy beseiged the walls of the village, and none of its inhabitants dared emerge. Such tunnels have been found, some of them of great size and representing remarkable engineering feats, in Trans-jordan in a place such as Shobek, and in Palestine in places such as Megiddo, Lachish, Gezer, and Jerusalem. All things considered, the best possible site then would be on top of a hill, commanding a spring or well or stream by or near which a road passed.

VI

Naturally, even if a site were ideal from the point of view of general situa-tion, protection, and water, unless it had some economic background, be it agricultural, commercial, industrial, or based upon religious needs, a village would not be located there in the first place. Assuming, however, that some general or particular reason had called a settlement into existence, it would usually, particularly during the first two periods in question, be located on a hill or some rise in the land, however small. In the course of time, the first village built on top of a hill, and surrounded by a fortification-wall, would be destroyed, either by an earthquake, or by a fire which may have broken out accidentally or as the result of an enemy attack. When, sometime after the destruction of the first village, another group of people wanted to build another village in its place, they would be compelled by the very conditions which determined the location of the first village, to build the second one on exactly the same place.

The newcomers had a choice of either digging up and removing the debris of the first village, and beginning anew from the same foundation levels, or of leveling off the ruins they found, and building above them an entirely new walled village, which was the usual practice. Just why this latter procedure was adopted instead of the former is difficult to say. The street levels of the Old City of modern Jerusalem are in some places approximately 25 meters above the level of the first structures built on the site. It is possible, for instance, to enter some of the churches in old Jerusalem, descend several flights of steps, and come down finally to the Roman level. A series of such staircases leads down thus through the Church of the Sisters of Zion to the pavement of the Praetorium (Antonia) of Pontius Pilate. If one were able to make a gigantic cross-section of old Jerusalem, it would be possible to see the accretions of many civilizations superimposed each upon the preceding one.

The practice of thus building one village upon the ruins of the preceding one led in the course of time to the formation of an entire artificial city-hill, within which might be concealed the ruins of five or ten or more villages or cities built one on top of the other. When such a hill of destroyed cities was finally abandoned, even the houses of the topmost and last city having been overthrown and covered with debris, it became known as a *tell*. And as a *tell* it is known in the Arabic vernacular to this day. Such a *tell* may be likened to a small skyscraper, each city in it being comparable to a separate floor. Already in Biblical times such artificial city-hills, neglected monuments of destroyed civilizations, must have strewn the landscape. The Prophets speak of a place becoming " a *tell* forever, an everlasting ruin."

At Tell Beit Mirsim, which is to be identified with the Biblical Qiryath-sefer or Debir, an expedition of the American School of Oriental Research at Jerusalem in conjunction with the Pittsburgh-Xenia Theological Seminary, dug through, or rather successively stripped off fifteen settlements built during the course of some 1600 years, each on top of the ruins of the preceding one. At Ezion-geber (Elath), first constructed by Solomon under the name of Ezion-geber as a seaport and industrial site on the north shore of the eastern arm of the Red Sea, another expedition of the American School excavated five settlements, built successively on top of each other. The artificial mound which they formed in the course of time is known today as Tell Kheleifeh. Its entire history extended through a period of about 500 years.

VII

The competent student of archaeology is possessed of a means which enables him, even before the spades of the diggers have exposed one after another the various levels of occupation contained in a *tell*, to estimate fairly accurately how many centuries have elapsed from its beginning to its end. On the basis of surface finds alone, he can tell with no more error than a hundred years in a thousand how old or how young a particular ancient site may be. The key to this knowledge is his acquaintance with ancient pottery. Many of the objects made of wood, or cloth, or leather, or parchment, or metal, or other perishable materials, have turned to dust and ashes together with the houses and towns in which they were contained when these were destroyed. Much of whatever by accident escaped this fate, disappeared sooner or later into a rusty patch or a wooden smudge, or not even that, as a result of the corrosive or decaying action set up when rain or subsurface water came into contact with these objects.

This is true, of course, particularly in such countries as Palestine and Transjordan, with their alternating rainy and dry seasons. In a country such as Egypt, where dry sands form an amazing protective cover, even such objects as fine linens and delicate woodwork can survive the passage of the millennia comparatively undamaged. In Palestine and Transjordan, however, one of the things which are essentially indestructible is the intensely fired and thoroughly baked clay pottery. Hundreds and thousands of such pottery jugs and jars and plates may be found more or less intact in the excavations, and many more smashed into fragments, but at least the fragments survive. And the archaeologist who is thoroughly acquainted with the ceramics of the country he is working in, can tell from characteristic fragments of pottery alone what period in history they belong to.

It was Flinders Petrie who toward the end of the last century first recognized the extreme value of these apparently insignificant potsherds. By carefully gathering them, together with unbroken vessels, from their respective levels at Tell el-Hesi in Palestine, he was able to date them approximately by the levels they were found in, and by the datable objects found with them, such as scarabs, and inscriptions, and jewelry, and coins. Soon in other excavations of similar places in Palestine, it was found that related examples of pottery, complete or broken, could always be dated by similar or comparative data to the same periods. Particularly since the close of the

1914-18 War, the study of Palestinian pottery has advanced so far and become
so refined, that for some years the expert has been able to pick up fragments
of pottery, let alone complete specimens, in excavations, and date them even
without other comparative materials. Indeed he can frequently use the
pottery as a criterion for dating other objects found with the pottery.

And more than that, merely by examining the fragments of pottery almost
always to be found on the tops and slopes of the artificial city-hills, even
before excavations have commenced, the archaeologist can give a fairly
accurate date for the history of all the settlements contained within any
one *tell*. As the winds blow or the rains wash soil away from the surfaces
of a mound, thousands of fragments of pottery of all the periods represented
in it are exposed to view. To the archaeologist or archaeological explorer
these potsherds are worth their weight in gold. To see them is to read
much of their history without the necessity of the written word.

A number of years ago, while undertaking an archaeological survey-expe-
dition through southern Palestine, William F. Albright came across an
ancient mound, mentioned above, called Tell Beit Mirsim. Climbing up
and down the slopes of the mound, he collected hundreds of fragments of
pottery which belonged to all the layers of ruined villages contained within
it, and on the basis of these surface finds alone came to the conclusion that
the site had been inhabited from about 2000 to about 600 B. C. Thereafter,
commencing in 1928, four successive years of excavations were carried out
there under his direction. On the basis of the great quantity of archaeological materials of all kinds obtained in the long and wearisome and most
carefully conducted excavations, Albright came to the conclusion that his
first estimate of the total history of the occupation of the site was mistaken.
No, Tell Beit Mirsim had not been inhabited from 2000 to 600 B. C. It had
been inhabited from 2200 to 586 B. C. In other words, the conclusions he
had arrived at on the basis of mere surface pottery finds were in general
completely corroborated by the results of the actual excavations. They were
merely made more exact.

Even more important than in Palestine are pottery finds in Transjordan
as an aid in recovering lost civilizations. In Palestine one finds a multiplicity of artificial " skyscraper " hills, with countless potsherds on and
around them. These *tells*, more properly *tulul* in the Arabic plural, are
formed on the principle explained above, because of the fact of a continuity
of history lasting from the early part of the Bronze Age, and sometimes
earlier, all the way down, in some instances, to the Byzantine or mediaeval
Arabic period, that is, generally speaking, from the 3rd millennium B. C.

or earlier down to about the 5th or the 12th century A. D. In Transjordan, however, south of the Wadi Zerqa, that is in the areas thus far archaeologically explored by the American School expeditions, there is a general absence of *tulul*. This was caused by the apparently almost complete absence of permanent settlements in stone villages and cities during intervals of many consecutive centuries, the land in the meantime being occupied for the most part evidently only by Bedouins.

For the present, it has been possible to establish the presence of two outstanding civilizations in the explored part of Transjordan during its early history. The one is the early Bronze Age civilization. The other is the Iron Age civilization. Between these there was a gap in the history of permanent sedentary occupation, lasting from about the end of the 20th to the beginning of the 13th century B. C., another gap extended from about the end of the 6th to the beginning of the 3rd century B. C. As a result, there was no chance for artificial city-hills to be formed, containing the ruins of settlements whose total span of history in some instances would have exceeded 3000 years.

In much of Transjordan, therefore, there are to be found as a rule only the ruins of sites, whose history lasted frequently less than five centuries, a period evidently not generally long enough for the formation of a *tell*. When such sites were destroyed and abandoned, their remains were not preserved under the protective covering of a superimposed mound, and in many instances were almost completely swept away by the ravages of time and the depredations of man. In all instances, however, the potsherds remained. Even in places where not a single stone of an ancient structure is visible above the surface of the ground, and where furthermore the ancient site has been ploughed over for generations, and all that is visible to the casual eye is a rough field, still careful search reveals there the presence of mutely eloquent pieces of pottery. These are extreme examples, but they occur with a degree of frequency in Transjordan which makes the archaeological explorer walk very warily indeed in places where for some of the reasons previously mentioned it might be expected that ancient sites were once located, and yet where at present there seem to be only barren wastes or torn up fields.

A case in point would be the discovery of Tawilan, an important Iron Age Edomite site situated immediately between the modern Arabic village of Elji and the entrance to Petra, the place known to most people as the great center of Nabataean civilization in southern Transjordan. As a result of previous archaeological finds in Petra proper, it had been possible to

equate the great fortress of Umm el-Biyarah (Fig. 5), on an inaccessible
mountain top in Petra, with the Biblical Sela.[4] That, however, was not
sufficient. We felt that there simply had to be somewhere in the environs
of Petra, if not within Petra itself, a large Edomite site, comparable to but
by far the superior of the modern village of Elji. There the Edomite farmers and trades-people would have lived, utilizing the strong waters of Ain
Musa (the spring of Moses) and the other springs in the vicinity, tilling

Fig. 5.   Umm el-Biyarah in Petra.
(Courtesy of the Palestine Department of Antiquities).

the fertile fields round about and inside of Petra, and engaging in the
caravan traffic which converged on Petra.

For many weary days in succession, we searched not only the Petra area
proper, but particularly the outskirts of Petra, and especially round about
Ain Musa. Again and again, at intervals during a period extending over
several years, we returned to the same area for further examination of the
hills and valleys in this region, convinced that a large settlement must have
existed there during the Iron Age, and another one before that during the

[4] I Chron. 2, 55; Jer. 35, 6-10.

Fig. 6. Edomite sherds from Tawilan (except Nos. 2-3 which are, respectively, from Khirbet Shedeiyid and Khirbet Nahas).

early part of the Bronze Age. Finally, one hot afternoon, we found some fragments of pottery which were indubitably Edomite, and thought that our search had finally been crowned with success. Still in vain, however. Hunt as we did, we could not find more than about five potsherds, on a hillslope which was distinctly unfavorable for the location of any ancient or modern site, although it was situated almost directly above Ain Musa. And even if we had found these sherds on a favorable location, it would have been impossible to maintain with certainty that they represented the remains of the large Edomite settlement that we believed must have existed near Ain Musa, at the entrance to Petra. After all, five sherds might have been brought there by an early relative of Job for the purpose of scraping his sores with them! The search continued.

Late one afternoon, while returning from the hills of Petra to Elji by a track we had not previously used, we stumbled across the site we were looking for. An archaeological explorer becomes in the course of time something like a hunting dog with his nose to the ground sniffing out scents. While walking across a field, immediately outside Petra and northeast of Elji, we saw some potsherds and mechanically stooped to pick them up and examine them. They were Edomite! Further examination showed that a large area was literally covered with thousands upon thousands of fragments of Edomite pottery, which could clearly be dated to the period extending between the 13th and the 6th centuries B. C., with the most important period of occupation, to judge from the frequency of the sherds, lasting from the 13th to the 8th centuries B. C. (Fig. 6).

The place is called Tawilan today. It is a completely ploughed up area, situated on a shelf of land immediately above the well irrigated gardens of the modern Arabic village of Elji, and below the high hill which rises above it, called Jebel Heidan. It was on the far side of this hill that we had previously found the above mentioned five fragments of Edomite pottery. No other Edomite site which we examined yielded as numerous or as varied types of pottery as did Tawilan (Fig. 7). Located between the springs of Ain Musa and Ain Sidr, and the Siq (the famous entrance to Petra), which it dominates, Tawilan proved to be the largest Edomite center in the entire Petra area. The fortress of Umm el-Biyarah in Petra served the military needs of the Edomites in this region and dominated the tracks leading down into the Arabah. Situated in the heart of a fertile, well watered area, which was thickly settled in the Edomite period, and located at a meeting point of important trade-routes, Tawilan was one of the most important centers of the Edomite kingdom. The passage in Amos 1, 12 referring to Bozrah and

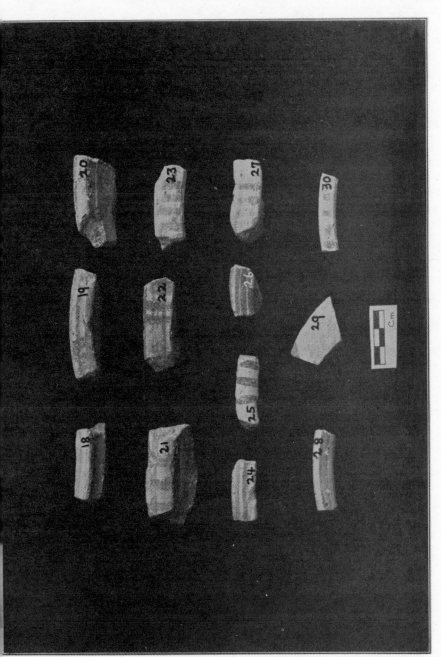

Fig. 7. Fragments of pottery rims from Tawilan.

Teiman as being evidently in the northern and southern parts of Edom, respectively, suggests the relative positions of Buseirah, which is to be identified with the Biblical Bozrah, and Tawilan, which is to be identified with the Biblical Teiman.

The discovery of the Edomite center of Tawilan is a somewhat extreme, but by no means isolated example of how ancient and long forgotten sites may be recovered through modern archaeological exploration, especially through the means of pottery identification. In earlier archaeological surveys of Transjordan and other countries the ancient sites which could be identified as such were for the most part those which had outstanding ruins. It is not an accident that archaeological studies of Transjordan until a few years ago dealt mainly with Roman antiquities and with Nabataean Petra and a few similar monumental places, while other antiquity sites which were recognized as such were merely designated as being ancient. Still others were passed over as of no significance, and many more were not known to exist.

As a result, large areas of Transjordan had, until recently, long been considered to be permanent waste lands, or indeed, if once inhabited in early times, to have been stripped of their populations by a gradually growing lack of rainfall, enabling desert conditions to penetrate farther and farther into once fertile areas. It has now been shown, as a result of pottery finds on hundreds of sites in the abandoned areas in question, that there were recurrent, though separated phases of extensive settlement there, to which we have already alluded. These widely separated periods of sedentary occupation belie the theory made popular by Ellsworth Huntington of an increasing diminution of rainfall and corresponding dessication in Transjordan and related parts of the Near East. The abandonment and reoccupation of entire countries such as Edom and Moab, for instance with gaps of centuries of complete lack of permanent, sedentary occupation between the two phases, cannot be explained by popular theories of precipitation cycles rendering human habitation in these areas progressively impossible. Although all the variables which make for the development and disappearance of populations cannot be established for such countries as Edom and Moab, or other ancient lands, the explanation both for the periods of intensive settlement and for those of extended abandonment of these countries is to be found rather in strictly human, more particularly in political and economic factors than in climatic changes.

Increasingly large areas in southern Transjordan are being occupied today by a sedentary population because of the newly established public security and improved economic conditions there. The Negeb of Palestine, for instance, could be made as habitable today as it was in the Byzantine period, were it settled by a population gifted with the courage, ability, and determination of its former inhabitants, other economic and political conditions being approximately equal. In a word, wherever in Edom or Moab or Ammon or Gilead or southern Palestine, sedentary populations have existed during various periods in the last four millennia, usually on or near the very same sites, it is still possible for villages and towns to spring up again. The climatic conditions have changed little if at all. And thus knowledge of ceramics can have direct bearing upon a much disputed climatic theory.

VIII

In addition to his knowledge of pottery in vogue in centuries gone by, and the previously mentioned aids, the archaeological explorer is helped in other ways also in finding ancient Biblical sites, and fixing the boundaries of Biblical lands. Very frequently descriptions of locations of cities or of boundaries mentioned in the Bible will be so exact that there can be no question of where they are situated. It is also not an uncommon occurrence to find the name of a Biblical city preserved down to this very day. One thinks immediately, of course, of such a name as Jerusalem, but there are many other examples. The Biblical Punon in the Wadi Arabah, where the Israelite hosts rested during their exodus from Sinai, is known today as Feinan. (The Arabs cannot pronounce the letter " P," and change it either into a " B " or an " F." Thus " pie " becomes known as " bie," and the Biblical Punon is changed to Feinan.) The Wadi Arabah is the Biblical Arabah. In Transjordan, the Biblical city of Aroer is known today among the Arabs as Arair, Dibon as Dhiban, Heshbon as Hesban, and Rabbath-Ammon as Amman. In the case of these particular names, the modern Arabic name clearly recalls the Biblical name, and in each case it can be proven that the correct site is thus designated. Sometimes, however, a modern place name may sound like a Biblical name, and yet have no connection whatsoever with the actual ancient site. Other times, ancient Biblical names are transferred in the course of time to sites to which they do not actually belong. It behooves the student of the Bible to be careful therefore in the use of modern place names for the identification of ancient Biblical places.

IX.

After a country such as Transjordan has been archaeologically explored and mapped, the time has come for some of the most promising of the ancient sites to be excavated. The work of excavation is a very slow, pedantically careful process, requiring much planning and labor (Fig. 8). It has to be done with scientific thoroughness. The entire site is usually divided into squares of varying size so that the architect on the expedition's staff can plot on his plans the lines of all the walls, and even at times the position of all the small finds that emerge from the excavations.

Traveling from Palestine to New York recently, one of the passengers on board ship and I engaged in conversation, during which he informed

Fig. 8.   Sorting pottery at Ezion-geber.

me that he was in the excavating business, and asked me what I did. I told him that I also was in the "excavating business." "I use steam-shovels in my work," he said, "and what do you use?" "Sieves," I replied. And that is literally true. Steam-shovels and other modern machinery would destroy or smash beyond recognition the ancient walls which have to be carefully disentangled from the debris in which they are buried, and the pottery and the other objects found with them. It is not an uncommon procedure in excavating to run all of the dirt and debris found in some of the rooms through sieves in order to catch the smallest objects, which may be of the greatest cultural importance (Fig. 9).

The laborers who do the actual digging, and the boys and sometimes the girls and women who carry the debris away, are given a reward for every object they find, in addition to a regular daily wage. Sharp watch is kept therefore by all for the minutest objects. A fine seal might easily bring its finder double or triple his daily wage, or even more. When objects made of gold are found, they are weighed and the finder receives the equi-

Fig. 9. Sifting debris at Ezion-geber.

valent of its value as gold bullion. These measures insure, in so far as is humanly possible, that all the objects found get into the hands of the scientific staff of the expedition and not into the pockets of antiquity dealers. As carefully as the laborers might be and are watched, it would be impossible, short of employing diamond-mine procedure, to prevent them from carrying off some of the finds, if it were not made worth their while to turn them over to the proper people.

The archaeologist is governed in his choice of a site to excavate by 1) the general location of the site, 2) whether or not there is a roadway or track over which supplies can be transported, 3) whether or not there are workmen in the vicinity, and 4) enough water to supply all needs, and particularly 5) by the nature of the site itself. He may be interested in the Roman period and will therefore dig a site in which he is certain to find traces of Roman civilization; or he may be particularly interested in a mediaeval Arabic site, or in an early Israelite one. Of course, it is not always possible to pick out the type of site to suit the particular interests of the individual archaeologist. If he is interested in a *tell* (of which type of antiquity site, to be sure, but few are to be found in Transjordan in contradistinction to Palestine), because of its importance in Israelite history, it may be necessary first ,of all to excavate Arabic, Byzantine, Roman, and Hellenistic cities, counting from the top down, before reaching the Israelite levels.

If the archaeologist is a careful one and proceeds in his excavations according to strictly scientific methods, he will treat the levels above the Israelite cities as carefully as the Israelite levels themselves. Each *tell* or other antiquity site is like some very valuable historical document. Even if one is interested only in part of it, the necessity is still taken for granted of treating the entire document very carefully. To destroy the topmost three levels in a *tell,* in order to reach the fourth with as little delay as possible, would be very much like tearing out the first three chapters of a book, in order immediately to get to the fourth chapter. Furthermore, it is never possible to say beforehand just what may be found of the utmost importance in a *tell* in levels belonging to a period earlier or later than the one the individual archaeologist may be especially interested in. Generally speaking, each level or settlement which it represents was influenced by the one that preceded it, and somehow or other was bound to influence in turn the settlement that was built on its ruins. The archaeologist's search for " buried treasures " may be directed, but must never be wantonly destructive.

Modern Biblical archaeology is certainly not a haphazard hunting for antiques. " Buried treasures " for the archaeologist do not necessarily mean hoards of precious metals or heaps of valuable jewels. A treasure may be represented by a single fragment of pottery on which an important name or date has been inscribed; or by the nature of a fortification wall; or by a pottery or metal figurine of a deity; or by an imported vase or scarab or piece of ivory. Furthermore, Biblical archaeology is essentially catholic in scope, and covers practically all the periods of history in Bible lands, and all of the prehistory that has thus far come to our knowledge. Many of the stages of prehistory and history in greater Palestine we know only in outline form. It will not be long certainly, to judge from finds in all fields of archaeology in Palestine and Transjordan during the last few years, before much of that outline is filled in. We do not yet know how the prehistoric inhabitants of the caves in the Wadi Mugharah near Haifa, and their contemporaries elsewhere in Palestine and Transjordan, influenced the peoples who came after them, who in historic times are found to be living in Palestine, but it may be taken for granted that they did. The archaeological research expeditions and excavations of the American School of Oriental Research, Jerusalem, have been concerned especially with periods from prehistoric times down to and through the days of Roman rule, and to a lesser degree down to the mediaeval Arabic period.

X

As for the Hebrews, whose history has been and still is most incomplete, archaeological finds in Palestine and surrounding countries have added enormously to our knowledge. The chief source of information, the Bible, is deficient in exhaustive objective historical facts. It is not a book of history, as we understand that term today. It is essentially a theological document presenting a specific religious point of view, namely that all the world and everything in it are the emanation of the divine will, being governed by divine purpose. The facts that serve to substantiate this central thesis have been retained frequently in full detail, at other times only in barest outline, and often meanings have been read into them. Other facts have been omitted completely.

A king, according to the editors of the Bible, is great or small, good or bad, depending upon whether or not he conforms to that which they believed was proper in the eyes of the Lord. Thus an Asa, a Josiah are praised and acclaimed; [5] yet the surrounding civilized world seems to have taken no cognizance of them. An Omri, however, the builder of Samaria, the new capital-city of Israel, is dismissed with a few sentences because he did not serve Yahweh properly.[6] His fame, however, had spread so far and was so enduring that in Assyrian annals, written long after his death, the kingdom of Israel is known as the land of Omri; [7] and the Moabite stone informs us of his Transjordanian conquests.

The religious, national, and personal ideals proclaimed and furthered by prophet and priest, and believed by them to be divinely inspired, are the

[5] I Kings 15.
[6] I Kings 16, 23-29; 20, 34.
[7] Barton, *Archaeology and the Bible*, ed. 6, p. 462.

4

primary concern of the Biblical narrative. Movements and individuals and folk-ways flash across the screen, and are judged in accordance with preconceived notions. The daily life of the people, the environment they moved in, the cultural influences they were subjected to, and the historical forces which directed them must frequently be gleaned and inferred from the Biblical records, and are too often lost in their bias or silence. Archaeology becomes the handmaid of history. The ground in which entire civilizations have been buried can be made to reveal its secrets.

Chapter II

THE DESERT OF EASTERN TRANSJORDAN

I

Before the 1914-18 War, a railway line ran all the way from Damascus to Medina, mainly to serve the needs of Mohammedan pilgrims on their way to the most sacred city of Islam. During that war, T. E. Lawrence and his associates roved up and down the length of the railway most assiduously dynamiting long stretches of track, innumerable culverts, and as many enemy trains as they could make contact with. After the close of the war, the railway line was repaired as far south as Ma'an in Transjordan, but beyond that it still lies as Lawrence left it, a broken length of twisted steel rails and blown-up bridges and culverts and wrecked stations. It has been left that way, because the astute king of most of Arabia, Ibn Saud, prefers to have it so. It becomes almost insuperably difficult now to throw troops and supplies against him quickly from the north, in any possible war that might be waged against him from that direction. He prefers the peace and the poverty of the trackless desert to the commercial benefits which might accrue to him from the restoration of the railway through the center of his kingdom. He would rather make most of his money from mineral and oil concessions to Americans who must enter his territory from the south.

For long stretches, the desert in Transjordan may be said to begin several kilometers west of the railway, but on the whole one can fix the boundary in Transjordan between the Sown and the Desert by the line of the railway. During the early historic periods in Transjordan, the inhabitants of the land were not able to penetrate much beyond that line. It is interesting to note that the eastern frontier fortresses of Edom and Moab and Ammon, for instance, are situated on the tops of high peaks of the chain of hills that borders the desert. The desert caravan routes and the spring grazing possibilities must also have been utilized to a certain degree by the inhabitants of these kingdoms during the Iron Age, but they had no permanent settlements in the desert. It was only from Nabataean times on that civilized peoples found it possible to reside there in stone buildings. In order to live in the desert, one must be graced with all the lack of needs that characterizes the true nomad who can and must follow his flocks from place to place, or with the capabilities of cultured peoples conversant with the intricacies of water engineering. The knowledge of how to conserve the natural water supplies has enabled groups to survive in the Transjordanian desert, where other sedentary groups less trained in the arts of life must have miserably perished had they tried to emulate their ways.

The desert is not to be thought of as consisting altogether of billowing sands. Most of it is hard, burnt-out sandy soil, with much of it covered by thin sheets of lava, formed in earliest prehistoric times, and now broken into millions upon millions of small fragments. For kilometers on end the landscape is black with myriads of lava pieces glistening in the sunshine with a brilliance that blinds the unaccustomed or unprotected eye. Driving over these lava covered areas makes an automobile sound like the proverbial bull in the china shop. Once while driving through a long stretch of this black, forbidding area, we saw ahead of us in the distance a large patch of green, a welcome sight for sore eyes. Surely a small oasis! Soon we reached the patch of green and the patch of green began to hop all over us. It was composed of a tremendous group of locusts.

The desert is, however, not always difficult and forbidding. After the spring rains, the grass springs up as if by magic, and the brilliant brownness and blackness is softened and hidden for a while by at first a sheen and then a carpet of green. Pools of water collect in hollows and depressions of all kinds, and remain for a while in parts of dry *wadi*-beds. Then the Bedouins appear with their flocks, which graze till the last blade of soft grass has disappeared and all the water is gone, and they are forced to bring them to better lands over which they have or take the right to roam. It must have been springtime when the Israelites, refused permission to travel through Edom and Moab, were compelled to go eastward around these countries and find their way through the desert. Only at this season of the year could man and beast in large numbers have found sufficient water and grazing to survive the rigors of the way.

II

During December 1932, a joint expedition of the Transjordan Department of Antiquities, and the American School of Oriental Research at Jerusalem, undertook a long trip of archaeological reconnaissance through the desert of eastern Transjordan from Mafraq to Kilwa. Mafraq is a station on the north end of the Transjordan railway, and was the headquarters in Transjordan of the Iraq Oil Company for the laying of the oil pipe line. Oil is being brought from the fields in Mosul to Haifa and Tripoli. Mafraq, whose very name indicates that it is a cross-roads point, was occupied in ancient times, as indicated by the rather enigmatic ruins of a large rectangular enclosure, measuring approximately 40 by 65 meters, to the northwest of the station-house. Only parts of the walls, built of large, rectangular, roughly dressed basalt blocks, are left. The stones are certainly not Roman, and the building-complex is probably to be assigned to a much earlier period, perhaps that of the Iron Age. The way from Mafraq led after a journey of more than 35 kilometers to the ruins of Qasr Hallabat, on top of a high knoll (Fig. 10). En route we passed parts of the Trajan highway, traveling first through flat desert and then through a rolling countryside dotted here and there with small hills. Below the hill of Qasr Hallabat was a huge, empty *birkeh* (reservoir), and a number of large cisterns.

Fig. 10.   Qasr Hallabat.

Reservoirs and cisterns such as these explain why in the past sedentary occupation was possible in the desert and in the semi-arid regions of Transjordan, where today not a single village or a solitary house is to be seen for miles around. There is today, farther south along the railway line, a police-post at the railway station of Ziza. By Ziza is a large, probably originally Roman reservoir, which the modern Transjordanian Government has cleaned out and repaired. One strong rain at the beginning of the rainy season, and the reservoir is full. It supplies not only the needs of the police-post, but of an entire village that has grown up beside it, in addition to the needs of the wayfarers who pass by, or the shepherds who come from considerable distances to water their flocks there. It seems possible that if all the ancient reservoirs and cisterns in Transjordan were cleaned out and repaired, the prosperity of the land and its population would immediately be greatly increased, and opportunity opened up for developments which would enable the country much more easily to rise to the glory which crowned it during several separate periods of history in the past.

On one occasion, early in the morning, we rode up to a village on the crown of a hill, noticing several ancient cisterns on the way up. Alighting from our horses, we asked the first man we met, in accordance with custom, to water our horses for us. He replied that there was no water in the village. Considering that incredible, we asked to be directed to the village chieftain, and repeating the request to him received the same answer. It soon turned out that this village of several hundred souls was actually altogether without water at the time of our arrival in the morning, because the women who had gone to fetch water had not yet returned. They were compelled to trudge to a spring apparently almost a kilometer away. Yet not a hand was lifted in the entire village to assure at least a reserve of water by cleaning out and repairing one of the ancient cisterns. It was obvious that if the inhabitants had opened up all of the ancient cisterns, and replastered them, they would have had after the first heavy rain a sufficient amount of water to take care of their limited needs for months on end.

At Qasr Hallabat itself there can be distinguished three different construction periods. The earliest structure seems to have been a small square castle made wholly of limestone blocks. It has been assigned to the earliest period of Roman military influence in the province of Arabia, i. e., to the reign of Trajan or Hadrian. However, it may be even older, and originally have been a Nabataean fortress. A fragment of a Nabataean funerary inscription was found there. The farther we penetrated southward into the desert along this eastern side of Transjordan, the more did the widespread nature of the Nabataean occupation become apparent. The Romans certainly controlled the desert, but the Nabataeans before them seem to have occupied it even more so. The Romans took over from the Nabataeans many of the fortresses and military outposts they left behind them when conquered by Trajan, although, to be sure, the Romans themselves built large numbers of military posts and fortresses anew.

The second period of Qasr Hallabat was marked by its being changed into a larger square castle, with towers at the four corners. Limestone and basalt blocks were used in its construction. A Latin inscription found there enabled it to be dated to the 3rd century A. D., in the reign of Caracalla, being built by the imperial legate Phirnius Julianus. The third building period could be dated there by a Greek inscription to the time of Justinian under the dux Flavius Anastasius in the 6th century A. D. The restorations of this period were completely of basalt blocks. Into one of the basalt walls of an interior room in the northern wing of the castle of the Justinian period was inserted a limestone block, decorated with two birds facing each other (Fig. 11). It probably came from the second period of construction of Qasr Hallabat belonging to the Caracalla period.

Immediately adjacent to the south side of the castle are the ruins of a smaller square structure, of excellent workmanship, built of smooth limestone blocks. It is generally considered to be a mosque, comparable in style to the 8th century A. D. Omayyad buildings of the nearby Hammam es-Sarakh and the farther distant Qeseir Amra. Around three sides of the so-called mosque were built arcades of semi-circular arches carried on piers. Only the bases of the piers are now to be seen among the ruins of the arches. Of interest is the curiously cusped window above the entrance in the west

Fig. 11.   Decorated building block from Qasr Hallabat.

wall (Fig. 12). The two capitals flanking the inside of the entrance in the west wall, each of which supports the springstone of an arch, suggest according to Butler " the capital with exaggerated abacus that belongs to the Nabataean period in Petra, Bosra, and Si'." It may well have represented a distant continuation of Nabataean artistic tradition, even as in general much of Omayyad art can clearly be traced back to Nabataean originals. This can be seen most clearly by a comparison of the sculptures and reliefs of the Nabataean temple of Khirbet Tannur in Transjordan with those of the Omayyad castle of Khirbet Mefjer north of Jericho in Palestine. It is thus interesting to note the multiplicity of cultural forces which can be traced in one fairly isolated place along the edge of the desert in Transjordan, such as Qasr Hallabat. Nabataean, Roman, Greek, and Arabic inscriptions and buildings, testify to the dynamism of all these forces, which pushed their advance posts out into the desert during their heyday, and in

one way or another left traces of their being behind them, not the least of
which consisted in the influence each, respectively, exerted upon the successor to power.

One of the most interesting castles we visited in the Transjordanian desert
was the one called Qasr Kharaneh. It was first visited in 1901 by Musil,
who also discovered and described Qasr Tuba and Qeseir Amra. Situated
on the caravan route leading from Amman to Medina via Teima, it was

Fig. 12.   Annex to Qasr Hallabat.

probably built by one of the early caliphs of the Omayyad dynasty at the
beginning of the 8th century A. D. Preserved in comparatively good state,
its distinctive Mesopotamian architecture differentiated it from the other
Omayyad castles in Transjordan. It is built approximately in the form of
a square, measuring 26.50 by 34.45 meters. Circular towers at each angle,
and a semi-circular tower in the center of each wall, with the exception of
the front south wall, accentuate the fortress-like appearance of the castle.
The towers are, however, primarily ornamental. The entrance in the south
wall is flanked by two ornamental quarter-circular towers. The walls are
constructed of rows of badly squared stones, with lines of small stones
between the rows, all of them set in mortar. The faces of the walls were
then plastered with a thick layer of mortar, some of which still remains,

especially on the east side. When the walls settled, this outer covering cracked along the lines of the stone layers. A very effective ornamental band of several rows of bricks placed at an angle of 45 degress upon each other, runs all around the building. The same zigzag type of brick decoration is repeated on each tower. Inside the castle, two stories of vaulted rooms are built around a practically square court. Interesting architectural features in a number of the rooms are the groups of three small columns against the walls, on which the arches rest which support the vaults of the ceiling. Between the groups of columns are large niches surmounted by semi-circular arches, decorated with saw-tooth, dentilated indentations.

Fig. 13.   Qeseir Amra.

There were also some very interesting rosette decorations sunk into the walls. Some of these latter features of decoration may very well go back to Nabataean inspiration carried over the intervening centuries.

Another one of these Omayyad castles is called Qeseir Amra (Fig. 13), about 8 kilometers east-northeast of Qasr Kharaneh, and about 42 kilometers southeast of Qasr Hallabat. It is a small hunting lodge and bath-house closely resembling Hammam es-Sarakh. Built, luxuriously equipped, and fantastically decorated probably by one of the early Omayyad princes at the beginning of the 8th century A. D., it served as a place of residence in the springtime. The effete princes of Damascus could never forget their desert origin, and were seized often with unconquerable nostalgia for the desert whence they had come, and to which they would return frequently for lengthy stays during the springtime. Qeseir Amra served some of them as a place of residence during this time of year. From there they started out on hunting trips, returning to rest and amuse themselves with poetry, astronomy, philosophy, and wine, women, and song. They gazed during hours of rest on ceilings decorated with paintings of dancing bears with musical instruments, and fat nudes, among others of similar type. The less important personnel lived in tents, or in simple stone barracks near by. The love of the Omayyad princes for the desert can be readily understood. It has a varying beauty all of its own, to which many from other climes are little sensible. In the early morning and particularly in the late afternoon it has a soft, sensuous beauty which is enthralling. The fierce light of the high sun then softens, until all the harshness and sharp wrinkles disappear from the landscape, with everything blotted out when night falls suddenly like a blanket thrown over a bird-cage.

Less than 30 kilometers east-northeast of Qeseir Amra is the strategically situated Qasr Azraq, where today is located one of the small, grim frontier posts, by means of which the Transjordan Government keeps the Bedouins in check. A few kilometers beyond it is the ancient fortress of Qasr Azraq, located among a few palm trees and surrounded by a multitude of springs, emptying into extensive marshes stretching to the southeast of it. Qasr Azraq is a large enclosure about 80 meters square, with towers at the four corners. Basalt was used throughout in its construction. It is dated by an Arabic inscription above the main gate to the 634th year of the Hegira, i. e. to 1236-7 A. D. That the Qasr was preceded by a Roman structure built on the same site is attested by an inscription on a basalt block found in the courtyard, dedicated to Diocletian and Maximian. Qasr Azraq is of particular importance because it guards the north end of the Wadi Sirhan, one of the main highways leading into the heart of the Arabian desert.

The Wadi Sirhan is a well watered rift or depression through the desert, furnishing a natural caravan route from Syria to Arabia. There is no evidence, but it seems most likely that it must have been used as such from early prehistoric times on. It is now a part of the territory of Ibn Saud, king of Arabia, and no possibility has presented itself as yet of exploring its length from the archaeological point of view. It is still used as a caravan route, but not nearly as much as we believe it was during one ancient period in particular, namely the Nabataean period. If it were possible to explore the Wadi Sirhan, there would present itself, we think, the complete explanation for the amazing development of the Syrian part of the Nabataean kingdom. This part, considered completely by itself, would be a good deal of an enigma. There would be found in all probability along the length of the Wadi Sirhan a line of Nabataean stations and caravanseries and police-posts similar to those found along the length of the somewhat similar Wadi Arabah, between the Dead Sea and the Gulf of Aqabah. The Nabataean caravans with their precious loads from Arabia could have followed the highway of the Wadi Sirhan to Syria as naturally as similar caravans followed the tracks through Arabia to southern Transjordan, and in part through the Wadi Arabah, whence they led either to Petra or westward to Gaza and Egypt. The Nabataean trade through the Wadi Sirhan to Syria led directly, it may be assumed, to the establishment in southeastern Syria of a, separate part of the Nabataean kingdom.*

A glance at the map of Syria, Transjordan, and Arabia reveals immediately that the most direct connection between the southern Transjordan and Syrian parts of the Nabataean kingdom lay through the independent territory of the Decapolis Union. The highway leading through this territory was indeed used by Nabataean caravans, but it could never have served as a life-line between the two parts of the Nabataean kingdom. This connection, were it the only one or even the main one, could easily have been cut off, bringing disaster to the important part of the Nabataean kingdom situated in Syria. The Nabataean occupation of southern Transjordan was more widespread and intensive, apparently, than the Nabataean occupation of southern Syria. Both, however, were natural developments of direct connections with Arabia. If we understand the Nabataean settlement in the Hauran and Jebel Druze regions of southern Syria as the natural consequence of its geographical relationship to the Wadi Sirhan, then the relationship of the two widely separated parts of the Nabataean kingdom in southern Syria and southern Transjordan becomes more understandable than hitherto. They were divergent parts of Nabataean Arabia, and it mattered not, therefore, that they were separated by the territory of the Decapolis Union. Whatever might happen to Nabataean traffic passing through this territory could not vitally affect either. Southern Transjordan could not be separated from Arabia; southern Syria must have been directly connected with it through the Wadi Sirhan.

Between Qasr Azraq and the important Nabataean desert outpost of Bayir (Wells) lies Qasr Tuba. It is about 70 kilometers southwest of Qasr Azraq, and about 50 kilometers east, east-northeast of el-Qatrani on the railway. It was originally built in the form of a rectangle measuring 140.50 by 72.85 meters, enclosing numerous vaulted brick chambers (Fig. 14). The outer walls of the enclosure are still fairly well preserved, with round towers at the four corners. Originally, there seem to have been five semicircular towers on the south side, and two, respectively, on the east and west sides. Against the center of the north side is a large, semi-circular tower, on each side of which is an entrance to the enclosure. Qasr Tuba could not have been meant to be a strong fortress. It seems to have been a station for passing caravans, as well as a spring residence for some Arab prince. The similarities between the forms of construction and ornamentation of Qasr Tuba and Qasr Meshetta have been variously pointed out. The problem of dating the two places is not yet solved. They are attributed by some to the Omayyads, by others to the Lahmides or the Ghassanides.

III

The Nabataean occupation of the eastern desert of Transjordan is illustrated at no place better than by the ruined Nabataean fortress at Bayir, which is about 87 kilometers southeast of el-Qatrani, and about 70 kilo-

Fig. 14.   Vaulted chamber at Qasr Tuba.

meters south-southeast of Qasr Tuba, and about 120 kilometers south-southwest of Qasr Azraq. Situated on an important desert crossroads, there is a modern Transjordan border fortress there today for the same reason that there was a Nabataean one there about 2000 years ago, to police this important traffic center, to keep the roads open, maintain public security, serve as a forepost to fend off possible Bedouin raids into the fertile areas, and to function as a halting place for caravans. The most important reason for the existence of a modern fort at Bayir, as well as for the existence of settlements there in the past, is contained in the name of the place, which means wells. There are two main wells in the plain below the modern fort, which is situated on a small hill. They are quite deep. A few years ago these wells were fixed up in modern fashion by the Transjordan Government, the tops being cemented over to prevent debris and refuse of all kinds from falling or being thrown in, and were equipped with modern gasoline pumps, the fuel being furnished by the government. The pumps soon got out of order. Lawrence having taught the countryside how to use dynamite, the cement coverings of the wells were blown off in short order, and the Bedouins returned to the time-honored practice of lowering a leather bucket, and then hauling up the rope hand over hand or hitching it to a camel or a donkey and driving the beast forward.

Near these wells are the very fragmentary remains of an ancient castle-fortress, rectangular in shape, with towers at the corners and against the walls. The castle had evidently at one time been built somewhat on the same plan as Qasr Tuba. It is not at all impossible that the present outline of the ruins may indeed be the remains of an Omayyad castle. That there was once, however, a much earlier castle or fortress on the site is indicated by the large number of Nabataean sherds found round about it, exactly like the Nabataean sherds found at Petra, for instance, and at the hundreds of other Nabataean sites visited by the American School expeditions in Transjordan. The Nabataean castle of Bayir and its successors were situated on the crossroads of tracks which led, respectively, southwest to Petra and then south to the Red Sea, west across the Wadi Arabah to Gaza or to Alexandria, southeast to Teima and Medain Saleh, and east to the Wadi Sirhan and Jauf. Arabic sources mention a desert track which led from Amman to Teima via Bayir.

IV

Another very important crossroads in the desert is located at the south-easternmost corner of Transjordan. It is called Kilwa, and is situated at the bottom of some of the hills of the Jebel Tubaiq. It is approximately midway between Aqabah on the north shore of the eastern arm of the Red Sea on the west, and the important oasis of Jauf to the east in Arabia. A direct track leads also southeastward from Amman via Bayir and Kilwa to Teima, another oasis in the Arabian desert. Kilwa is about 130 kilometers southeast of Bayir. The existence of ruins at Kilwa was known to us even before our arrival there, because Gertrude Bell had mentioned them in her *Letters,* p. 273. She had done little more than that, however, but it was sufficient to arouse our curiosity as to the real nature of the ruins she had seen. She seems to have been the first European to have visited them, having passed them on her way to Hayil in 1914. A most unexpected sight met our eyes as our expedition arrived at Kilwa. Situated at the side of a small, dry *wadi,* in a rough sandy plain covered with basalt

pebbles and boulders, and surrounded by the gloomy hills of the Jebel
Tubaiq, was an ancient settlement, with the ruins of a number of houses
still standing. The main group of buildings at Kilwa, constructed of
basalt blocks, resembles in general type the stone buildings of the southern
Hauran of an earlier date. A cistern, a shallow *birkeh,* and the remains
of several wells indicated how the small population of the site had obtained
its water supplies during the year. The entire number of inhabitants could
never have been more than a hundred, and probably a good many less than
that during most of the year.

Fig. 15. Arabic inscription with a Maltese cross on a lintel over a
monk's cell at Christian Kilwa.

To judge from the crosses (Fig. 15) and Arabic inscriptions at Kilwa,
and also from the nature of a number of small cells immediately north and
east of the several small buildings, it seems most probable that Kilwa was
the seat of a small monastic settlement, which can be dated to about 1000
A. D. At the top of one of these cells was a large stone slab with an Arabic
inscription, at the right of which was a Maltese cross. The letters which
are badly worn have been read as follows: " in the name of God . . . made
this . . . cell." Before the advent of Mohammed, orthodox Christian her-
mitages lay on the main caravan routes. The monks lent aid to the
travellers and tended the sick. Also after the advent of Mohammed,
Christian tribes and settlements are known to have lived in amity with
their Moslem neighbors, even though at times they appeared, so to speak,
to be tiny islands situated in great seas. The Christian community at Kilwa

must be thought of in this wise, and indeed its presence along the crossroads of the desert in the Jebel Tubaiq must have been welcomed because of the Samaritan nature of its interests.

Several hundred meters east-northeast of the buildings and cells of the monastic settlement, lies a small, Nubian sandstone hill. Our attention was drawn to it by reason of the fact that at the base of it were several small constructions, which upon closer examination turned out to be lime kilns, obviously contemporary with the buildings of the monastic settlement.

Fig. 16. Prehistoric rock-drawing of a large ox superimposed on two earlier
rock-drawings of ibexes. Below a stylized figure of a man
perhaps thrusting a spear into the side of the ox.

They were made of basalt blocks, and incorporated corbel features of construction exactly like those of the larger buildings. The lime prepared in these kilns was used for plastering the faces of the main buildings, although none seems to have been used as mortar between rows of stones of the buildings. A further examination of the hill, however, revealed to our amazement that every smooth surface on it was covered with prehistoric rock-drawings, some of them superimposed upon one another. Gertrude Bell had completely missed them, but they must have been familiar to the early Christian inhabitants of the site. With the exception of several members of the Transjordan military force, we were the first westerners with scientific interests to see these rock-drawings, which testified to the presence of prehistoric man in this remote corner of the north Arabian desert.

One of the most interesting of the rock-drawings on this hill, and the only one of its kind, is that of an elongated, narrow-headed, horned animal, presumably an ox, over two meters long, superimposed over several smaller and previously incised drawings of ibexes (Fig. 16). Just like small children who draw one picture on a slate, and then draw another on top of it, and a third inside of it, so also in early prehistoric times, and naturally not only at Kilwa, did the artists of the day draw one animal after another

Fig. 17.   Prehistoric rock-drawing of a wounded ibex.

in the very same space. The head of one of these drawings may be seen protruding below the tail of the larger animal, and another crude horned animal may be seen portrayed within the lines of the body of the larger animal. Under the ox, with his arms raised above his head, is the highly stylized representation of a human-being, depicted in squatting position, characteristic of other prehistoric rock-drawings of human figures found in Spain and Africa. This representation particularly resembles one from the Fezzan rock-drawings in North Africa. In one hand, the prehistoric man of Kilwa seems to be holding a spear, which he is thrusting into the side of the ox. The composition evidently represents a hunting scene. There is no question but that the ox and the representation of the human figure squatting under it are contemporary, any more than there is a question but that the two very crude drawings of ibexes over which the drawing of the ox has been superimposed belong to a different, and in all probability somewhat earlier period.

Not all of the rock drawings on this hill are as crude as that of the ox and man and ibexes. One of the most beautiful of the drawings, is that of an ibex standing by itself (Fig. 17). It has an attractiveness of line and form that requires no comparative judgment. It is about fifty centimeters high, and is faithfully and artistically rendered. The burin marks are clearly visible, the lower left end of each stroke of the flint chisel being slightly deeper than the upper end. Some of the lines were obtained by chiselling from either edge of the desired width of the line, the deepest indentation being in the middle. The prehistoric artist possessed considerable ability. The full beauty of the delicate animal, which incidentally is still to be seen in the Transjordanian desert, has been caught and imprisoned in the lines on the stone. Nostrils and neckline, horns rising and sweeping back gracefully from the head, then curving and tapering to sharp points touching the back, the foreleg lifted in movement,—all these features bound together in a delicate yet strongly portrayed whole give the rock-drawing a vibrant reality, which seems somewhat strange in view of the thousands of years which have elapsed since it was first executed. The head of the ibex is raised, and from its mouth stream two lines which may possibly be meant to represent streams of blood. If that is correct, we might have here a picture of a wounded ibex poised in flight.

On top of this ibex, hardly visible at times in the brilliant sunshine that plays on it during most of the day, is the crude drawing of a small human figure with outstretched arms. The lines of this small drawing are much more shallow than those of the main drawing of the ibex proper, the workmanship quite different, and the whole drawing so obscure or obscured by the passage of time, that it can easily escape detection, even by the eye of the camera in some lights. We believe it belongs to an entirely different period, namely to the Thamudic period in the 3rd century A. D., to which period other rock-drawings and inscriptions on this sandstone hill of Kilwa belong. There are numerous other rock-drawings of ibexes of varying degrees of attractiveness and preservation (Fig. 18).

Of much interest is another rock-drawing representing a human pair in seated position, clasped together in close embrace. This was discovered by another archaeological expedition, which visited Kilwa several years after we had been there. It is very similar to the limestone statuette found by Neuville in the Wadi Khreitun near Bethlehem, which he assigned to the Natufian period. Another rock-drawing at Kilwa seems to represent at first glance a male figure seated within a double circle. Closer observation

5

shows that there is an entire confusion of rock-drawings contained in this group. What seem to be the lines of a double circle are actually the lines of a pair of ibex horns, all that remain of the original drawing of an ibex which may have looked much like the one described above. The rest of the lines of this particular ibex have been completely weathered away, a fate that has befallen many of the original rock-drawings. The outlines of what appear to be a male figure reveal themselves actually to be those of two very crude little animals, drawn sidewise with limbs touching.

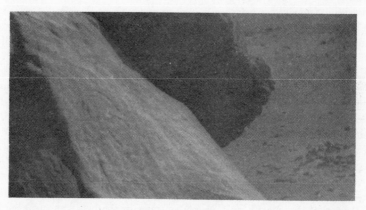

Fig. 18. Prehistoric rock-drawing of an ibex.

There are many other drawings at Kilwa on this very same sandstone hill, which obviously belong to a much later period than those thus far dealt with, namely the Thamudic period of the 3rd century A. D., to which we have alluded. The lines, patina, and the entire manner of execution are different. A considerable number of these later rock-drawings are so directly associated with Thamudic inscriptions that it becomes impossible not to date them to the Thamudic period. On the basis of the rock-drawings alone, we were inclined originally to assign the prehistoric ones to the end of the paleolithic and the beginning of the neolithic periods. However, we had no time during our visit there to hunt for flints or fauna by means of which this dating could have been substantiated or changed. Our means of dating was by comparison with other rock-drawings found in Africa and Spain. We did not even try to return to Kilwa at a later date for a more prolonged examination of the site, during which we could have worked at our leisure, but rested content in publishing as much as we had seen, and the conclusions we had arrived at on the basis of our finds. As a result of the finds of a German expedition, it seems proper to date the earliest of the rock-drawings, among which we include the ox with the squatting human figure and the graceful ibex, to the Mesolithic period, beginning with Nutufian I, and carry the history of the rock-drawings and the flints found in the environs down to the Ghassulian or Chalcolithic period, that is, covering a span of time from about the beginning of the 10th millennium down to about the first half of the 5th millennium B. C.

It is naturally of profound interest to the student of ancient history in Transjordan to know of the existence of this prehistoric center, and to obtain some idea of the nature of the prehistoric man who wandered about in this region, living evidently a nomadic existence, and depending for his sustenance on the hunt. It is also interesting to note that this hill remained a center of assembly for the nomads even down into early Christian times when, in the 3rd century A. D., rock-drawings were still being chiseled and drilled there. The desert of eastern Transjordan we see is not empty of history. It has been pulsating with the life of man for many millennia. Wherever there are routes of travel, crossroads of traffic, water-holes furnishing some possibility of existence, animals that could be hunted for food, areas where at least during certain times of the year flocks could graze, there men and their belongings assemble, and frequently leave behind them some trace or other of their sojourn upon the face of the earth, even if it be in the desert. At all events, the desert in eastern Transjordan must be accounted a rich province for those who are interested in ancient history, and in particular in the backgrounds of the Biblical world. It is essentially a frontier land, into which during historic times the advance posts of thriving agricultural civilizations have been thrust forward, and from which in turn the Bedouins, seeking ever for openings in the bulwarks of the defences thrown up against them, surge forward in quest of loot and land.

CHAPTER III

KING SOLOMON'S COPPER MINES.

I

Comparable to the desert of eastern Transjordan in interest, but if anything surpassing it in importance, is the Wadi Arabah. A great rift between the Dead Sea and the Gulf of Aqabah, it forms a dividing line between southern Palestine and southern Transjordan. It is a part of the tremendous geological fault, which is continued southward by the Gulf of Aqabah, the eastern arm of the Red Sea, and northward by the Jordan River Valley, and by the Beq'ah between the Lebanon and the Anti-Lebanon mountains. It is in every sense of the word a waste land, which for all practical purposes remains completely unoccupied today. One may travel throughout its entire area for long periods on end, without meeting more than a few Bedouins. It is really only in springtime that life seems at all possible in it, and it is during that period of the year that the Bedouins drive their flocks down there to graze on the short-lived grass and herbage that spring up after the winter rains. Along its entire length there are comparatively few water-holes, some of them as far apart as a good day's journey by camel. It is only at several places along the edges of the *wadi* that there are substantial supplies of water, such as at Feinan on the east side and at Ghadyan and Ain Hosb on the west side (Fig. 19). And it is only at Feinan that a small area, irrigated by the water of the stream that flows continuously from the hills of Edom, is cultivated. The only group of people in the past that cultivated the soil at fairly many places even in the Wadi Arabah were the Nabataeans. Wherever in this wasteland there was any water whatsoever, there they tilled the soil over considerable areas.

At et-Telah, where today there is a small spring of water, is situated an amazing Nabataean site. It consists of the ruins of a large *birkeh*, reservoir, in which water was stored, conducted there by a long conduit leading from the source of the spring up a *wadi* leading down from the hills of Edom (Fig. 20). Some distance below the reservoir are the ruins of a large caravanserai, and below it there spreads an amazing area of square, walled fields, watered in ancient times by a spreading system of irrigation ditches branching off from a main channel leading from the reservoir. When viewed from the air, the wide spread of once carefully cultivated fields, each of

50

which was surrounded by strongly built stone walls, looks like a huge checker-board (Fig. 21). A kilometer before arriving at et-Telah, it was possible to identify the site as Nabataean by the countless fragments of Nabataean pottery strewn over the surface of the ground; and, similarly, Nabataean sherds can be found in large numbers on the ground for about

Fig. 19. Ain Hosb.

a kilometer beyond the present extent of the walled fields. The laboriously erected walls served the purpose of protective terracing, keeping the soil of the gradual slopes on which they were located in place even during the periods of the heavy winter and spring rains. So excellently was the work done that after a lapse of about 2000 years large areas of the terraced stretches of walled gardens are still intact, with the walls almost perfectly

preserved, and the soil as ready for cultivation today as it was near the
beginning of our era. Only the sections of garden walls directly in the
spreading path of the waters of the *wadi* in spate have been swept away
during the passage of the centuries. There are several similar places in the
Wadi Arabah, such as one east of Qasr Feifeh nears its north end, composed
of two walled compounds (Figs. 22 and 23), where in like fashion the Nabataeans demonstrated their ability to wrest a living even from marginal lands.

Fig. 20. Southwest corner of **Birket et-Telah.**

No people before the Nabataeans, and none since their time has been able
to emulate their example in the Wadi Arabah, and in places such as et-Telah
cultivate the soil. And yet we know that the Wadi Arabah was of supreme
importance to every group or nation that aspired to or obtained control of
Palestine or Transjordan. For the Nabataeans, as for the Romans who
succeeded them and transformed their kingdom into a Roman province, the
Wadi Arabah was primarily of great value because it served as an important highway between Palestine and Transjordan, leading also to Arabia
and Egypt. In addition to the sites already referred to, there were numerous
other Nabataean and later Roman caravan stations all along the length of
the Wadi Arabah.

For the peoples that preceded the Nabataeans and Romans, however, particularly for the Israelites and Judaeans on the one hand and the Edomites and Moabites on the other hand, this bleak and bare wasteland was of even greater importance than for them. At intervals during a period

Fig. 21. et-Telah.

(Courtesy Air Officer Commanding, Royal Air Force, Middle East).

of about two hundred years, war was waged between the Edomites and the Israelites and later on the Judaeans for the mastery of this area. A problem that long awaited solution was the discovery of the impelling reason for the bitter struggle, partly as a result of which both sides fought themselves practically to a position of mutual exhaustion. Certainly in the case of the Edomites, the resultant weakness must be considered as one of the contributing causes for their disappearance as a separate ethnic and political group, before the advance of the Bedouins who were to people their land for centuries. Most of these Bedouins left no trace of their stay behind them;

Fig. 22.   A Nabataean-Roman site east of Qasr Feifeh
(note line of aqueduct).

(Courtesy Air Officer Commanding, Royal Air Force, Middle East).

among them, however, came the Nabataeans, who in the course of time not only gained complete possession of the former territories of Moab and Edom, but also swung themselves in a few remarkable centuries from a nomadic to a highly advanced agricultural civilization.

Some idea of the specific nature of the importance of the Wadi Arabah in ancient times can be gleaned from the account in Numbers 33, according to which part of the way of the Israelites during the Exodus led through

the Arabah from Ezion-geber, at its southern end on the Red Sea, as far
north as Punon (the modern Feinan) on the east side of the Arabah.
From this and other Biblical stories, including those dealing with frequent
raids by the Edomites into Cisjordan via the Wadi Arabah, it is obvious
that, already in Israelite-Edomite times, it was frequented as an important

Fig. 23.   Another Nabataean-Roman site east of Qasr Feifeh
(note terrace walls).

(Courtesy Air Officer Commanding, Royal Air Force, Middle East).

route of travel. In addition, it has been known for some time as a result
of discoveries by Musil, Blake, Kirkbride, Head, and Horsfield, that mineral
deposits, particularly copper, existed there. To determine, therefore, the
exact lines of travel in ancient times in the Wadi Arabah, and to examine
more closely the few known mineral deposits there, a joint expedition of the
American School of Oriental Research at Jerusalem, Hebrew Union College,
Cincinnati, and the Transjordan Department of Antiquities, attempted in

the spring of 1934 a thoroughgoing archaeological survey of this rift. The expedition had not penetrated very far, before discoveries began to be made which were to afford much new information about the entire complex of problems connected with the Wadi Arabah in the past, and particularly during and immediately after the time of King Solomon.

II

About 30 kilometers south of the Dead Sea, the expedition discovered the remains of a hitherto unknown fortress, called Khirbet Hamr Ifdan. Situated on the top of an isolated hill, the fortress commanded the access to a small nearby spring, Ain Hamr Ifdan. Little is left of the acropolis except some sections of revetment on the north side. On the top of the west side of the acropolis are the remains of a tower, with some traces of room-foundations near the middle of the formerly enclosed area. At the foot of the acropolis hill are the remains of a long retaining (?) wall, while on the hillside immediately east of it are the remains of a walled enclosure. The acropolis hill rises precipitously about 30 meters above the *wudyan* that almost completely surround it. Numerous fragments of pottery were found on the top and sides of the acropolis hill, all of which belonged to the Iron Age, that is to the time of the kings of Israel and Judah, and particularly to the time of Solomon. To judge from the size and strength and stra-tegically located position of the fortress, Khirbet Hamr Ifdan must have been the seat of an important garrison. It was at first impossible, however, to determine just what function such a strongly fortified site, situated apparently in the midst of a bleak nowhere, could possibly have served. The spring was not large enough to demand the presence of a strong garrison to police the Bedouins, and to control the caravans which may have halted on occasion by its side. It certainly was not in the midst of a fertile farm area, that had to be protected against nomad invasions. The answer was soon obtained, however, in an altogether unexpected fashion, when it was discovered that Khirbet Hamr Ifdan commanded the roads leading to a number of very important mining and smelting sites a few kilometers away from it. Perhaps in relationship with Khirbet Hamr Ifdan may be placed another fortress, situated near the above mentioned Nabataean-Roman site east of Qasr Feifeh. We saw it only from the air (Fig. 24). It is on top of one of the foothills on the east side of the Wadi Arabah, and may well have served to guard the track leading through the Ghor Feifeh to the top of the Edomite plateau east of it. To judge from its general appearance and location, we would guess it to be a site contemporary with Khirbet Hamr Ifdan.

About six kilometers in a straight line east-southeast of Khirbet Hamr Ifdan, we came to a large ruined site called Khirbet Nahas, which literally translated from the Arabic means the *Copper Ruin*. Repeated questions

Fig. 24. Rujm east of Qasr Feifeh.

(Courtesy Air Officer Commanding, Royal Air Force, Middle East).

elicited no sensible replies from our Arab guides as to why the site was called by that particular name. They were well aware of its presence, knew indeed that the place contained a *khirbeh*, i. e. an ancient ruin, but had no idea whatsoever with regard to the origin of the name, except to repeat over and over again that it had been called so by their fathers. It must not be

concluded that our Arab guides were by any means stupid or uninformed
about things pertaining to their way of life. They could understand from
tracks days old who and how many people had passed on the way before
them; they knew the desert like a book; they could survive under conditions
which would have spelled disaster for others from so-called more advanced

Fig. 25. Sheikh Audeh ibn Ahmed el-Asfar of the
Beni Atiyeh tribe.

stages of civilization. Such a man as the chief of our guides and camel
men, upon whose skill and direction and knowledge of the Wadi Arabah our
expedition in many ways was completely dependent, Sheikh Audeh ibn
Ahmed el-Asfar of the Beni Atiyeh tribe (Fig. 25), who had met us with
nine camels and five members of his tribe, and accompanied us all the
way through the Wadi Arabah, was as courteous and fine a gentleman as I
ever met. He, and the others with him, simply had not learned how to

evaluate the small, seemingly insignificant archaeological data, which to the initiated meant as much as data dealing with trails and desert life meant to the Arab. For that matter, similar archaeological data have been completely passed over by western scholars who were not trained to perceive them, or to evaluate them even if brought to their attention.

Khirbet Nahas was what its name indicated it to be, a great copper mining and smelting site. The cupriferous ores surface mined in the surrounding districts were collected there, and put through an initial smelting or

Fig. 26. Smelting furnace at Khirbet Nahas.

" roasting " process. Khirbet Nahas is situated in an oblong cul-de-sac, pointed north-south. A semi-circular sweep of high sandstone hills encloses the site. On the east side is a small *wadi* which runs northwest to join the larger Wadi Gheweibeh, by the side of which, incidentally, we were to discover a related site. Between the hills on the south and west sides of Khirbet Nahas and the *wudyan* on the east and north sides lies a large flat area packed with ruins of walls, large buildings, miners' huts, and smelting furnaces, and black with great heaps of copper slag. Great quantities of cupriferous sandstone are visible in the immediate vicinity. Mining the ore was a simple task. Of particular interest are the numerous small ruined furnaces visible on the site, two of them near the south side, a square and a circular one, being still fairly intact. The first (Fig. 26), built of roughly hewn blocks, is 3 meters square, and has two compartments one above the other. The ruins of the furnace are now 1.50 meters high. The inside of the lower compartment measures 2.5 by .8 meters.

At the northwest end of Khirbet Nahas is a large enclosure, 76 meters square, with walls 2 meters thick, and it is oriented northwest by southeast. Part of the wall at the northwest corner is comparatively intact, being still 6 courses high. Elsewhere the long lines of its walls are marked by fallen heaps of masonry. The entrance is probably on the northwest side, completely blocked by piles of fallen debris, representing towers guarding the entrance on the inside. Within the enclosure are also the ruins of miners' huts and smelting furnaces, with heaps of slag between them. The enclosure makes the appearance of a large prison camp. It is probable, as we shall see also from similar sites, that the mines and smelting plants were manned with slave labor, both when the Israelites and Edomites in turn controlled the Wadi Arabah, and also in subsequent periods. Living conditions in the Wadi Arabah being what they were and are, the laborers who mined and smelted the copper were in all likelihood held to their tasks under compulsion whenever the mines were worked. It is interesting to note in this connection that in patristic literature there are numerous references to the copper mines at Feinan which were worked by slave labor, either of Christians or of criminals, condemned there for their convictions or their crimes.

At the present time there is very little water in the immediate vicinity of Khirbet Nahas. There is a small spring on the north side of Wadi Gheweibeh opposite it, which was, however, insufficient even for our own needs. Some springs may have dried up or been buried. Likewise no water whatsoever was found in the vicinity of the nearby mining camp of Khirbet Jariyeh.

Of particular importance were the quantities of worn potsherds found on the surface of Khirbet Nahas. Almost all of them were fragments of large, coarse jars and storage-pots of various kinds, such as one might expect to find in a rude mining camp, where much of the pottery used may have been locally made. Khirbet Nahas had been cursorily visited by Musil in 1898, and subsequently by Kirkbride, Horsfield, Head, and Frank. Frank collected some of the fragments of pottery strewn on the surface, judging them to be older than Roman. As a matter of fact, practically all of the pottery at Khirbet Nahas can be dated to the Iron Age. More particularly, the most important periods of activity there, to judge from the main masses of pottery fragments, were during and after the reign of

King Solomon. In the absence of all other documents dealing with Khirbet Nahas, these potsherds are of primary importance in enabling us to determine when the surface mines in the vicinity of the site were worked, and when the raw ores were "roasted" or partly smelted in the furnaces, with the resultant formation of the large slag heaps near them.

Khirbet Nahas was the center of a series of other mining and smelting sites in the vicinity. We do not feel that we have discovered all of them. The terrain is difficult to traverse, the *wudyan* twist about in the most unaccountable fashion, and we should have been compelled to spend perhaps weeks in this one area in order to discover all the mining camps which may exist there. When subsequently we flew over the area, hoping to locate more of these mining sites from the air, we were not even able in the time at our disposal to locate all of those we had already visited on the ground.

About 5 kilometers east-northeast of Khirbet Nahas, following the course of the Wadi Gheweibeh, we came to the spring of Ain Gheweibeh near the beginning of the *wadi*. The waters of the spring flow but a comparatively short distance before disappearing into the sandy bed of the *wadi*. A short distance above the spring, on the high ground on either side of the *wadi*, which had narrowed considerably at this point, lie the ruins of Khirbet Gheweibeh, which could be seen at first glance to be another mining and smelting site, smaller in size, however, than Khirbet Nahas. The fairly flat areas on either side of the *wadi* were dotted with the ruins of houses and small smelting furnaces, and were black with pieces and piles of slag. In the center of the northern half of this mining camp are the ruins of the foundation-walls of a building 10 meters square, perhaps the commanding officer's residence or the main watch-tower on the site, which seemed to be otherwise unfortified. On the surface of the site were found numerous fragments of pottery, most of which belonged to the same periods in the Iron Age as at Nahas.

But a few kilometers away from Khirbet Gheweibeh, and actually less than 3 kilometers north-northeast of Khirbet Nahas, we found another ancient copper mining and smelting site, called Khirbet Jariyeh. Like Khirbet Gheweibeh, Khirbet Jariyeh lies sprawled over two high, flat areas, separated by an intervening *wadi*, and almost completely encircled by hills. Musil visited the Jebel Jariyeh but did not get to Khirbet Jariyeh, and small wonder, because unless one were looking for such a site it could easily be missed, hidden as it is in a pocket between the hills. The two halves of the site are covered with ruins of houses and smelting furnaces and are black with heaps of slag (Fig. 27). The two main sections of the sites seem originally to have been enclosed with strong walls. The western half is divided into two parts by a tiny *wadi* running west-east through the center of the area into the Wadi Jariyeh. Two small smelting furnaces were found still fairly intact, a circular one at the south end of the east side, and a square one at the north end of the west side (Fig. 28), with foundations of other furnaces visible near the center of the west side of the site, and another circular furnace near it. The first one mentioned is in

Fig. 27.   Khirbet Jariyeh.

the form of an irregular circle and measures 2.9 by 2.6 meters; the square one is 2.70 meters square. These smelting furnaces are now only one story high. The roof of each was formed by placing several long, thin, rectangular stone slabs over the side walls, which are less than a meter in height and are built of three courses of rudely cut blocks of stone. Some of the smelting furnaces were two stories high, one compartment above the other.

Just how the ores were smelted or "roasted" in these small furnaces is unknown to us. Perhaps a bellows of some sort was used to keep the flames going, or perhaps the strong winds in the Wadi Arabah were used to form a natural draft on the principle that we shall see was utilized in the elaborate refineries in Solomon's port city and factory town of Ezion-geber.

The question of the fuel supply will be taken up shortly. Some of the larger buildings at Khirbet Jariyeh and other sites of similar nature visited in the Wadi Arabah may very well have been fairly large smelters, in which there were several furnace rooms. In Sinai, at similar copper mining and smelting sites, marked also by slag heaps, furnaces of various kinds have been found, none of them, however, in such comparatively good condition as

Fig. 28. Smelting Furnace B at Khirbet Jariyeh.

those in the Wadi Arabah. On the surface of Khirbet Jariyeh were found numerous specimens of good ore consisting of mixed cuprite and malachite, and also pieces of cupriferous sandstone. Numerous Iron Age potsherds were found giving the same dates arrived at from the examination of the pottery fragments of the other mining and smelting sites in the vicinity.

III

The problem of furnishing an adequate water supply for the mining camps must have been a difficult one for the operators to solve. It seems probable that all these copper-mining and smelting sites in the Wadi Arabah,

6

with the exception of Feinan where there is enough water for a sizeable community, were worked only during the winter and early spring, that is, during the main rainy seasons. It is also possible, that in some instances water may have been imported from long distances. However, careless of human life as the masters of the mines may have been, there still remained the pressing necessity of supplying comparatively large quantities of water to the personnel and the slaves engaged in the various branches of the work.

We know that in Sinai, food and water and fuel supplies were transported over long distances regularly to the mining camps from various centers where they were available. There, where to be sure the precious torquoise gems rather than the copper deposits were particularly sought after, the ancient mines were worked by annual expeditions sent out from Egypt during the spring. In connection with one of these Egyptian mining expeditions to Sinai, Egyptian records indicate that a train of 500 donkeys conducted by 43 peasants was used to maintain a steady flow of supplies of all kinds, including food and water, to the various mining camps. A similar organization, we believe, must have existed to take care of the needs of the mining camps in the Wadi Arabah. Food, fuel, and even water supplies in part must have been brought to such places as Khirbet Nahas and Khirbet Jariyeh by trains of camels and donkeys which returned laden with the " roasted " or partly smelted ores. To judge from the subsequent discoveries at Ezion-geber, it would seem that these partly treated ores were brought to be further smelted and refined and worked up partly into finished metal products at the smelters and foundries and factories of Ezion-geber, particularly during and immediately after the time of King Solomon.

The question of the fuel supply necessary to keep the smelting furnaces going in the various mining centers throughout the length of the Wadi Arabah presents at first glance serious difficulties. While food and, if necessary, water supplies could have been transported from many centers, the same could not be said of fuel supplies. It does not seem likely that there were any more fuel supplies available in the vicinity of these mining and smelting sites in the Wadi Arabah during the Iron Age than there are today. Considerable quantities of dry shrubs and bushes may have been gathered to fire these furnaces, just as today in Palestine and Transjordan many crude lime kilns are fired by bundles of such materials laboriously gathered together over comparatively long stretches of time. Large parties foraging over wide areas could assemble considerable quantities of such fuel even in the Wadi Arabah, although it would appear to be uneconomical effort, and in no event could it suffice to fire the furnaces regularly. At best, it would seem that the fuel obtained from the Wadi Arabah itself could hardly have been utilized for more than the ordinary cooking purposes of the various camps.

Most of the fuel was obtained in an altogether different fashion, we believe. It was probably imported in the form of charcoal, burned on the heavily wooded slopes of the hills of Edom, and then transported by camel and donkey to the various mining settlements in the Wadi Arabah. It will be remembered that the stands of wood in the hills of Edom were so extensive as late as the 1914-18 War, that the Turks built a special branch railway, leading off westward from the main north-south Bosra-Medina line, into the heart of the great stands of oak and cedar in Edom. Specifically, it ran from Jurf ed-Derawish, a station on the main line, to Ain Nejel below Shobek for the sole purpose of hauling out timber cut from the then still existing forests. Whoever wanders on foot from the hills back of Petra northward to Shobek must pass thousands of stumps of large trees cut down during this slaughter of great and beautiful forests. In as much as such forests never existed on the slopes of the hills along the western side of the Wadi Arabah, there could be no other supplies of fuel for the smelting furnaces fired so intensively in the Wadi Arabah during the Iron Age than from the once heavily wooded hills of Edom.

IV

That not all of the mining and smelting sites in the Wadi Arabah were restricted to the Iron Age period, and especially to and after the time of King Solomon, is indicated, for example, by Khirbet Neqeib Aseimer, about a kilometer south-southeast of Khirbet Nahas. It is situated at the end of a large *wadi*, oriented east-southeast by west-southwest, and is surrounded the hills. On the cross ridge at the west-northwest end of Khirbet Neqeib be another copper mining and smelting center of considerable size, evidently tapping the same area of cupriferous sandstone deposits, which had brought Khirbet Nahas into existence. On the slopes of the hills on the north and south sides, and in the flat area between them, were numerous ruins of dwellings and furnaces, with large and small slag heaps between them. There was a particularly large number of ruins of small buildings and furnaces on the south-southwest side near the top of the ridge. One of them was a peculiarly shaped building which looked like a bottle with a small narrow opening between two rectangular columns of masonry. It may well have been a large smelting furnace. Just how it looked on the inside could not be determined because of the mass of fallen stones.

There were the ruins of several large buildings in the small valley between the hills. On the cross ridge at the west-northwest end of Khirbet Neqeib Aseimer are the ruins of a large, irregularly shaped, more or less rectangular building, measuring 17.70 meters on the east side, 17 meters on the west, 9.30 meters on the south, and 11.10 meters on the north. The walls are preserved in some places to a height of nine courses, being built of roughly squared blocks of stone, with small stones between the rows, as at the Omayyad castle of Qasr Kharaneh in the Transjordan desert dating to the 8th century A. D. There are three horizontal partitions on the inside of the building, which divide the space into six compartments, serving originally perhaps as furnaces. Three windows are still visible, one in the north wall near the east end, one in the west wall at the south end, and one near the center of the south wall. There are small piles of slag inside the building and very large slag heaps in front of it. From the evidence offered by this building, it becomes apparent that many of the large buildings at Khirbet Neqeib Aseimer and elsewhere in these mining and smelting centers may have been smelters, housing a number of smelting furnaces under one roof. They may have been similar to the much larger smelters to be discovered later on at Ezion-geber. Numerous specimens of cupriferous sandstone and of mixed cuprite and malachite were collected.

To judge from the nature of the construction of the buildings at Khirbet Neqeib Aseimer, they would seem to be mediaeval Arabic in origin. They are certainly different from the building types found in the Iron Age mining and smelting sites in the Wadi Arabah. Neither Iron Age nor Nabataean sherds were found there, which is somewhat surprising in view of the proximity of Khirbet Nahas, where both of these types were found, but there were a number of mediaeval Arabic sherds (Fig. 29). We must conclude therefore that this site was occupied only during the mediaeval Arabic period. Feinan, which is less than 7 kilometers south-southeast of Khirbet Neqeib Aseimer, is the only other site in the Wadi Arabah, where mining and smelting activities were possibly carried on during this period.

This much, however, seems definitely certain. During no period were mining and smelting activities carried on in the Wadi Arabah as extensively as during the Iron Age. We have already referred to the fact known from patristic literature, that copper mines at Feinan were worked in part by early Christians condemned to slavery. Whether or not other copper mines in the Wadi Arabah were worked during the early Christian period is not known. It is not likely, for there is no evidence of the existence then of the intricate organization necessary for large scale production of copper and to a lesser degree of iron, which seems to have existed for that purpose during the Iron Age.

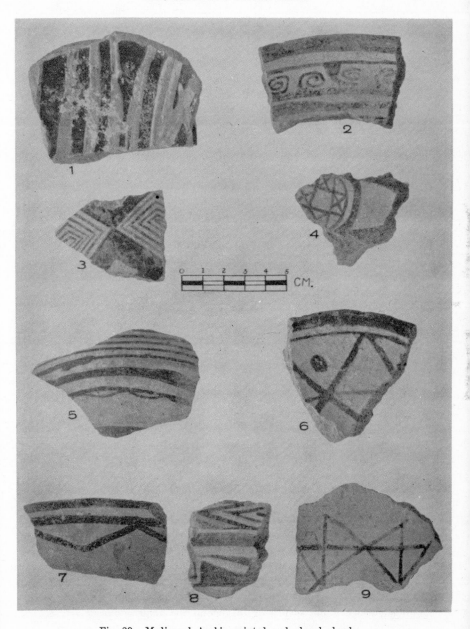

Fig. 29. Mediaeval Arabic painted and glazed sherds.

V

About 8.5 kilometers south-southeast of Khirbet Nahas, and less than 7 kilometers south-southeast of Khirbet Neqeib Aseimer, lies Feinan. It is a tremendous site, a large part of which is on the north side of the Wadi Gheweir, as the lower part of the Wadi Dathneh is called before it joins the Wadi Dana to form the Wadi Ifdan, which runs into the Wadi Arabah. There are also large ruins on both sides of the Wadi Sheqer, which coming from the south joins the Wadi Gheweir. All of these *wudyan* originate in the foothills of Edom immediately to the east of Feinan. An abundance of water flowing through the *wudyan* all the year round irrigates a large cultivated area, which, however, is smaller today than it was in the Nabataean period. To the east an important track leads through the ascending Wadi Dana to the highlands of Edom. As has already been pointed out, Feinan is to be identified with the Biblical Punon, one of the stations of the Exodus mentioned in Numbers 33, 42.

Immediately north of the Wadi Gheweir is a large hill which dominates the entire site. On top of it are the ruins of Khirbet Feinan, among which are included the foundation remains of several Byzantine structures. Immediately west of the hill is a ruined basilica. On the east, south, and southwest slopes of the hill were found pieces and heaps of copper slag, as well as numerous chunks of cupriferous sandstone. Musil reports seeing the shaft of a mine on the southwest slope of the hill, and Frank seeing there a circular smelting furnace 2.50 meters in diameter and 2.50 meters high. There are also copper slag heaps on the south side of the Wadi Gheweir. West of them are the ruins of a reservoir, a mill, and a connecting aqueduct, which apparently belong to the Byzantine period. Subsequently we discovered in the hills above Feinan, at a point between Shobek on top of the Edomite plateau and Feinan, an extensively worked mine called Umm el-Amad or Umm el-Awamid. Large quantities of copper ore were brought from there to Feinan to be smelted, we believe. The excellent water supply at Feinan enabled a considerable community to live there and carry on industrial activities.

A careful search for sherds was made over the entire site of Feinan, particularly on the top and slopes of the mound. A sufficient number was collected to establish the approximate dates of the various settlements. The pottery finds indicate first of all a sedentary occupation of Feinan from the end of the Early Bronze Age down to the first part of the Middle Bronze Age, that is, from about 2200-1900 B. C. Only a handful of such sherds was found, which is not surprising in view of the numerous large settlements built above this early Bronze Age site in subsequent centuries of occupation. There were, however, enough of these fragments of pottery to show beyond all doubt that during this period, the end of which is generally associated with the time of Abraham, a permanent settlement was located there. The next period of sedentary occupation of Feinan, to judge from the pottery found there, commenced in the 13th century B. C. and lasted down to about the 6th century B. C., in a word throughout the Iron Age. The subsequent period of permanent sedentary occupation, about three centuries later, belongs to the Nabataeans. From that time on, Feinan was almost continuously settled, being occupied in the Roman, Byzantine, and mediaeval Arabic periods, with some small settlements in modern times of a semi-sedentary character.

It seems fairly certain, in view of the proximity of Feinan to the other Iron Age mining and smelting sites described above, and in view of the similarity of its Iron Age pottery to that found at these places, that mining activities were carried on at Feinan during the Iron Age, and particularly during and after the 10th century B. C. It is possible also that copper was mined at Feinan and in the vicinity, and partly smelted there during the early part of the Bronze Age, to judge again from the fragments of pottery of that period found there. If so, it is the only place thus far discovered in the Wadi Arabah, or at any place in Palestine and Transjordan, where copper was mined and smelted at that time.

In view of the close relationship between Edom and Sinai, it is indeed remarkable that we did not find more copper mining and smelting sites which were worked about ± 2000 B. C. The mines of Serabit Khadim in Sinai had their first important development under the 3rd dynasty in the reign of Snefru, then a period of intensive exploitation under the 12th dynasty, and were reopened by the Pharaohs of the 18th and 19th dynasties. The possibility of the connection of Bronze Age Feinan with the contemporary sites in Sinai is heightened by the fact that the early Bronze Age trade route which we have been able to trace down through Transjordan seems to turn westward at Feinan, leading to Sinai.

Large quantities of Nabataean sherds were found at Feinan. Whether or not the Nabataeans engaged in mining and smelting activities there is difficult to determine. We know that the Nabataeans engaged in such activities on a large scale at Sabrah, about 7 kilometers south-southeast of Petra, as is evident from the extensive workings there. Small quantities of Nabataean sherds were found at Khirbet Nahas, Khirbet Gheweibeh, and Khirbet Jariyeh, but to judge from the great preponderance of the Iron Age sherds found at these places, the likelihood is that they were exploited for mining purposes during the Iron Age only. The Nabataean sherds may have come from herdsmen's tents or small police-posts, or from passing caravans. It is also difficult to determine whether or not the Romans engaged in mining and smelting activities at Feinan, although it seems likely that they and the Nabataeans before them did. There was a large Roman settlement there, as is indicated by the ruins of numerous Roman buildings, and by the presence of large quantities of Roman sherds.

That the Romans carried on mining activities in the Wadi Arabah has been demonstrated beyond all question by a Latin inscription with Greek additions above a Nabataean text scratched on a stone block, found at the "northeast corner of the Red Sea" by Frank. Mining and smelting activities may have been carried on at Feinan also during the Byzantine and mediaeval Arabic periods, when there were large settlements there. In view of the nearness of the large mining and smelting center at Khirbet Neqeib Aseimer, which flourished during the mediaeval Arabic period, it seems likely that similar activities were carried on also at Feinan during that period.

An important ancient copper mine was found among the hills east of Feinan, which mark the steep slope up to the top of the Edomite plateau. We started out from Shobek on top of the plateau in order to find it. Half an hour's walk from Shobek to the northwest through a rich agricultural region brought us to the edge of the plateau overlooking the Wadi Arabah, with the black looking range of the Jebel Hamr Ifdan looming up in it. Commencing the descent to the northwest in the general direction of Feinan, we passed through a wooded and grass-covered area, typical of the top of the western slopes of the Jebel Shera part of the Edomite plateau, which led down into the foothills overlooking the Wadi Arabah. As the descent became steeper, the cultivation became less and soon ceased altogether. Entering finally the Wadi Umm el-Amad, the descent became so precipitous that it was necessary to leave the donkey and our packs behind and clamber down the right side of the *wadi*, which we were told, runs into the Wadi Arabah immediately south of Feinan. After about three hours' walk, 12.5 kilometers west-northwest of Shobek we arrived at the ancient copper mine we had been looking for. It is called Umm el-Amad or Umm el-Awamid, the Mother of Pillars. Below it, approximately 8 kilometers to the northwest, is Feinan.

It was its name, "The Mother of Pillars," that suggested to us that it might possibly be an ancient mine. We had searched for it a long time and had been led on many false trails before finally finding a guide in Shobek who actually knew where it was located. The copper mine of Umm el-Amad was cut into the face of a sandstone cliff on the right side of the *wadi* of the same name. There are five large pillars at the entrance of the mine, which extends into the hill for about 35 meters (Fig. 30). At its widest point it measures about 19 meters. The roof inside the mine is supported by numerous free-standing pillars similar to those at the entrance. They average about 2.5 meters in height and about a meter in width. It is necessary to crawl through the entrance, where the debris of centuries is slowly mounting towards the roof. Inside, however, it is possible to stand upright. There are also the beginnings of a number of galleries visible at the far end of the mine, which were not followed up by

Fig. 30. The entrance to Umm el-Amad, looking north.

the early miners. The pick marks left by the tools of the miners are still visible on the walls and roof and on the pillars, all of which are black with smoke. Generations of nomads and herdsmen have camped in Umm el-Amad since it was abandoned as a mine, and they have left piles of debris under which sherds may be buried. Veins and nodules of ore are visible in the walls and pillars of the mine (Fig. 31). The cupriferous sandstone of Umm el-Amad, which is also speckled with iron oxide, was as we have already suggested, probably transported to Feinan to be crushed and smelted, because of the excellent supply of water available there. In as much as no sherds were found at Umm el-Amad, it is impossible to say definitely just when the mine was worked. It seems safe, however, to assume that it was certainly worked during the Iron Age, when most of the mining and smelting activities in the Arabah took place.

VI

The caravan route southward from Feinan to Aqabah leads past two ancient ruined sites, one known as Khirbet Bir Madhkur and the other as Khirbet Taiyibeh. Bir Madhkur is situated about 24 kilometers south-southwest of Feinan along the east side of the Arabah. Approaching it we

Fig. 31.   Pillars at entrance of Umm el-Amad
showing veins and nodules of ore.

passed through numerous, formerly cultivated fields strewn with Nabataean sherds. There are two large ruins by Bir Madhkur, one of them of a large caravanserai, and the other of what may have been a reservoir. Bir Madhkur itself is a deep well, originally lined with masonry, some of the cut stones of which are still visible. A number of shrubs and trees grow nearby. There is also a small spring. We found an extraordinarily large number of Nabataean pottery fragments of all types strewn all over the surface, and some Roman sherds and coins. We found nothing, however, which belonged to the Iron Age or to the early part of the Bronze Age.

The presence of this extensive site in the midst of the wilderness of the Wadi Arabah during the Nabataean-Roman period is characteristic at once of the industriousness of the Nabataeans and of their Roman conquerors. It also illustrates the difference between the Iron Age and the Nabataean

Fig. 32.   Bir Taiyibeh.

occupations of the Wadi Arabah. During the Iron Age it was important primarily as a source of minerals, and then as a route of travel and trade to and from the Red Sea. Mining camps were set up regardless of the location of springs. During the Nabataean-Roman period, however, caravanserais and fortresses were established at almost all of the water-holes.

About 9 kilometers southwest of Khirbet Bir Madhkur lies Khirbet Taiyibeh. There is a completely ruined Nabataean-Roman caravanserai there, by three water-holes, called the Biyar Taiyibeh, around each of which grew clumps of reeds (Fig. 32). Khirbet Taiyibeh is the southern counterpart of Khirbet Bir Madhkur, and like it guards a direct track to Petra.

Back of Petra, about 7 kilometers south-southwest of it, is an extensive Nabataean mining and smelting center at a place called es-Sabrah. About a kilometer west of the actual site of es-Sabrah we found large deposits of highly cupriferous sandstone, particularly at a point where the Wadi es-Sabrah widens out considerably. It is probable that there are other cupriferous sandstone deposits immediately in the vicinity of es-Sabrah. In addition, throughout much of the length of the Wadi es-Sabrah, we found numerous specimens and entire veins of very rich iron ore. On the north side of the *wadi*, immediately above the spring called Ain es-Sabrah, are

Fig. 33.   Theatre at es-Sabrah.

the ruins of a number of large buildings constructed of blocks of reddish sandstone. Some of the ruined buildings on top of the *wadi* embankment were evidently devoted to the smelting of copper on a large scale, to judge from the heaps of copper ore slag found by them. The largest of the copper smelting plants was at the western end of the groups of buildings on the north side of the *wadi*.

On the southeast side of the Wadi es-Sabrah, not far from these industrial buildings, are the well-preserved remains of a small theater, with many of the seats still in place (Fig. 33). Back of the top seats is a strong wall made of well-cut sandstone blocks. On these blocks can be seen the lines cut at a 45 degree angle by the Nabataean masons. The wall served as one side of a *birkeh*, whose other sides were formed by a semi-circular space behind it in the face of the hill. The rain water, pouring through an artificially enlarged cleft in the hillside far above the theater, plunged down the fissure in its side and was caught in the *birkeh*. The *wadi*-bed between the theater and the smelting plants was originally paved with rectangular sandstone blocks, some of which are still visible. Very large quantities of Nabataean sherds of all kinds were found among the ruins, indicating beyond all doubt that this mining and smelting site belonged to the Nabataean period, particularly between the 2nd century B. C. and the 2nd century A. D.

It is quite likely that the Romans continued to make use of this site for its original purposes when they succeeded the Nabataeans, taking over *en bloc* not only the Nabataean mines and buildings, but also the Nabataean workmen and the Nabataean pottery makers. The size and nature of the Nabataean-Roman mining and smelting center of es-Sabrah, which with its theater was a mining camp de luxe, lead one to think that had the Nabataeans and Romans worked the copper mines in the Wadi Arabah after the Edomites, they would have left a much more indelible impression of their presence and activities than has been found. It is surprising, in view of the known Edomite settlements in and near Petra, that no Edomite sherds were found at es-Sabrah. Possibly the large scale Nabataean-Roman operations there effectively removed all traces of former Edomite activities, although that does not appear to be likely.

The route we followed through the Wadi Arabah from Khirbet Taiyibeh led us south-southwest past Ain and Wadi Gharandel (Fig. 34), where near the spring we found the ruin of another Nabataean-Roman caravanserai, marked by some Nabataean sherds. The place, called Gharandel, was known in Roman times as Aridella. Crossing from there to the western side of the Wadi Arabah, and proceeding southward we came to a place called Hafriyat Ghadyan (Fig. 35). It is a large, circular earth-work about 70 meters in diameter, which seems to have been a crude dam. Its floor is lower than the surface of the surrounding plain. We found no pottery fragments whatsoever to give us a date of the occupation of the site, but did find numerous pieces of slag indicating that smelting operations had been carried on there at some time in the ancient past, and that there must be mineral deposits in the vicinity. Some specimens of cupriferous sandstone and of limonite (iron ore) were found on the surface.

A few kilometers farther to the south we came upon the ruins of a caravanserai at a place called Ghadyan. The importance of Ghadyan in the Wadi Arabah lies in the fact there is a large number of wells and springs there, with a practically unlimited water supply. They are at the northwestern end of a large mud flat that becomes impassable in the winter and

Fig. 34. Wadi Gharandel, looking west.

Fig. 35. Some of the expedition's camels grazing in the Wadi Arabah
at Hafriyat Ghadyan.

early spring during the rainy season. Some of the wells were dug through approximately half a meter of solid rock, while others penetrate several meters through earth and rock before the plentiful underground water supply is reached. Near them are some stone troughs. One strong spring has created a swampy area around it. The entire surrounding area is covered with coarse grass and reeds and bushes, which provide excellent grazing for numerous herds of camels and goats. A careful search around the caravanserai revealed only a few Nabataean sherds. There were also several pieces of slag. The caravanserai is very near the western foothills of the Arabah, and it was between it and the foothills that the sherds and pieces of slag were found. The ore deposits must be in the adjacent foothills. There were also some pieces of cupriferous sandstone on the surface of the site.

VII

Following the track south-southwest which mounted gradually on the Palestinian side of the Wadi Arabah, we came to the Jebel Mene'iyeh, a series of shale and reddish sandstone hills containing huge deposits of copper ore. Mene'iyeh is the largest and richest copper mining and smelting center in the entire Arabah. It is about 38 kilometers north-northwest of the northwest edge of the Gulf of Aqabah. Entering the Wadi Mene'iyeh from the north, after passing a small *rujm* which may have been a watchtower guarding the narrow entrance to the *wadi*, we came upon a typical mining and smelting center with about twenty furnaces and houses in an advanced state of ruin, between which were piles of slag. Numerous fragments of pottery were found, belonging to the Iron Age and particularly to the period of King Solomon and later. The same pottery finds were made in all the other mining camps located at Mene'iyeh, agreeing thus with the pottery finds north of it. About a hundred meters directly to the south was another such smelting center, with approximately the same number of furnaces and houses and similar heaps of slag and types of pottery. About 550 meters southeast of this we came upon a third such site, somewhat larger than the first two but built in the same way. Altogether we found seven such sites in the Mene'iyeh area where copper mining and smelting operations were carried on. Mining the cupriferous sandstone was a very simple task at Mene'iyeh because it protruded all over the surface of the entire *wadi*. We collected numerous specimens of mixed cuprite and malachite and of highly cupriferous sandstone.

Among these mining camps is situated Khirbet Mene'iyeh, a great

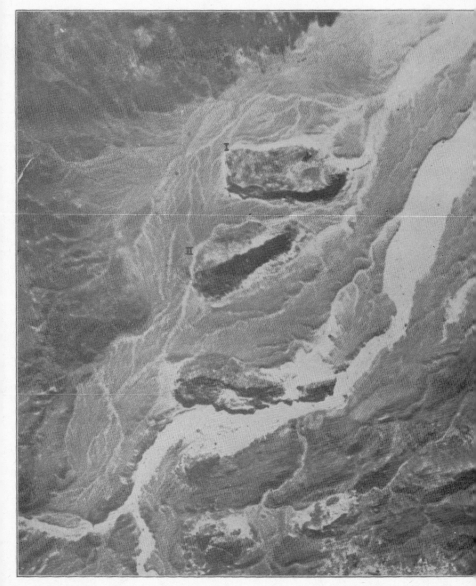

Fig. 36. Air view of Mene'iyeh, with wall and slag heaps visible on acropolis hill, marked "I" knife-edged hill marked "II" shows semi-circular walled enclosure below north end.

(Courtesy Air Officer Commanding, Royal Air Force, Middle East).

acropolis which not only served to guard them, but also protected the southern approach to the other mining camps in the Wadi Arabah. It was the southern counterpart of Khirbet Hamr Ifdan. The acropolis is built on top of a high, flat-topped, isolated hill, which rises sheer about 40 meters above the Wadi Mene'iyeh. The entire top of the hill was enclosed by a wall, parts of which are still preserved. The wall is made of rough sandstone blocks. Its original width could not be exactly ascertained but may have been about a meter and a half. The acropolis is oriented north-south and measures approximately 336 by 125 meters. At the northern and southern ends of the acropolis are small natural prominences, shaped somewhat like horns, on top of which are ruins of what may have originally been watch-towers. There are ruins of furnaces and other buildings within the acropolis area on top of the hill, together with heaps and innumerable pieces of slag, and large quantities of Iron Age sherds. The only feasible ascent to the top of the acropolis hill is from the southeast. The outer wall enclosing the acropolis, particularly on the west side, and also the black slag heaps, are clearly visible from the air. The walled, flat top of the acropolis hill of Khirbet Mene'iyeh seems also to have served as a prison camp, where the drafted laborers engaged in the smelting operations were forcibly detained (Fig. 36). There is a similar place at Khirbet Nahas.

On the west side of the *wadi*, opposite the acropolis hill, is another large, isolated hill whose top comes to a knife-edge. Below the north end of the hill is a semi-circular walled area. The ends of the wall, which are built high up against the steep sides of the hill, are 77 meters apart. Near the center of the northern side of this compound is an entrance, guarded by two ruined towers on either side of it. Inside the walls are the ruins of houses and furnaces and great heaps of black slag, much of which, as in the cases of all the other slag heaps at these mining and smelting camps, is spotted green with the remains of copper that were not refined out of it. There were also numerous fragments of Iron Age pottery. The nature of this place with its thick walls of masonry, now tumbled down, suggests that it too was used as a prison camp, in which the members of the corvée were held under compulsion to their arduous tasks (Fig. 37). We found no water in the entire Mene'iyeh area.

From Mene'iyeh the track leads southward through the Wadi Arabah past the spring of Ain Defiyeh (Fig. 38) to the shore of the Gulf of Aqabah. A few kilometers below the Palestinian police-post of Mrashrash, overlooking the northwest corner of the Gulf of Aqabah, we discovered another mining and smelting site, which may be called Khirbet Mrashrash. On the slopes and tops of two of the foothills which run down to the very

7

Fig. 37. Walled enclosure at Mene'iyeh, showing heaps of slag and ruins of smelting furnaces and miners' huts.

Fig. 38. Ain Defiyeh in the Wadi Arabah.

water's edge we found masses of copper slag (Fig. 39). No bits of pottery were found by these slag heaps, nor did we locate the source of the copper ore itself, which must be in the immediate vicinity. It seems reasonable however, to believe that these slag heaps go back to mining and smelting operations carried on during the Iron Age, to which period we have been able to assign most of the mining and smelting centers in the Wadi Arabah.

The discovery of Khirbet Mrashrash completes the line of such mining

Fig. 39. Copper slag near Mrashrash, on a hillside overlooking the northwest corner of the Gulf of Aqabah.

centers along almost the entire length of the Wadi Arabah. In as much as Frank has reported the discovery of pieces of slag, indicating the presence at one time of smelting furnaces; immediately at the southeast corner of the Dead Sea, it may be said that the mineral deposits in the Wadi Arabah extend all the way from the Dead Sea to the Gulf of Aqabah. We repeat that in all probability other mining and smelting sites will be discovered along the length of the Wadi Arabah other than those we have mentioned. It seems furthermore quite possible that the copper deposits in the Wadi Arabah are connected geologically with the known copper deposits in Sinai, and may well be part of one continuous formation. It is interesting to note in this connection that about 10 kilometers southwest of Mrashrash copper deposits have been discovered in the Wadi Tabah (Fig. 40), above the police station of Bir Tabah where there had been mines in ancient times.

Fig. 40. Ain Tabah.

(Courtesy of J. H. Iliffe).

Fig. 41. Ruins at north-northeast end of Jeziret Far'un.

Going about 8 kilometers into the interior through the Wadi Merah, which forms a large delta about a kilometer southwest of the island of Jeziret Far'un (Fig. 41) at the northwest end of the Gulf of Aqabah, Frank found copper deposits which had been tapped through pits and shafts. As in the Wadi Tabah, the ore seems to have been smelted elsewhere. A Nabataean inscription was found among these copper deposits.

VIII

The discovery of the datable mineral deposits in the Wadi Arabah has afforded us much information with regard to the ancient history of Israel and Judah and Edom. Long before the advent of the Israelites, the presence of the mineral deposits in the Wadi Arabah was known and the mines exploited in all probability by the Kenites and the Edomites, to whom they were related through the Kenizzites.[1] It was the Kenites, who were native to the country and whose very name indicates that they were smiths, and the related Kenizzites, many of whom also were smiths by profession, who probably first imparted to the Israelites and the Edomites information about the ore deposits in the Wadi Arabah; and who introduced the Israelites and the Edomites to the arts of mining and metallurgy. It will be recalled that Moses took a wife from the Kenites, and that the Israelites ever afterwards maintained the closest relationship with them. Was it from the Kenites that Moses learned how to make a copper serpent?[2] Saul was mindful of the close connection between the Israelites and the Kenites, and spared them in his battles with the Amalekites.

That the Kenites were at home in Edom and in the Wadi Arabah is indicated by Balaam's punning proverb with regard to them in Numbers 24, 21: "Everlasting is thy habitation, and set in the Rock (*Sela*) is thy Nest (*Qen*)." The pun on *Qen* and Kenite (Qenite) is obvious, and *Sela* is to be identified with Umm el-Biyarah in Petra. The Bible tells that Tubal-Cain (a Kenite) was the first forger of copper and iron instruments.[3] It is stated in Chronicles,[4] that the Kenizzites lived in the *Valley of Smiths*. We believe that this means the Wadi Arabah, with its many copper and iron mining and smelting sites, and that the *City of Copper* mentioned in connection with the *Valley of Smiths* is to be identified with the large Iron Age mining and smelting site of Khirbet Nahas (the Copper Ruin), located near the north end of the Wadi Arabah. Confirmed wanderers, the Kenites seem to have retained throughout their history a Bedouin form of life, like

[1] Genesis 15, 19; 36, 10. 11. 42.
[2] Numbers 21, 9.
[3] Genesis 4, 22.
[4] I Chron. 4, 12-14.

the related Rechabites and Jerahmeelites. The presence of individual
Kenites in Judah and Israel, pictured as wandering about from place to
place, can be understood when it is realized that they were itinerant smiths.

IX

The Wadi Arabah with its minerals, having also access to the trade of
Arabia and the commerce of the Red Sea, was, we believe, the main cause
of the bitter and protracted warfare between Israel and Edom. Israel was
wise enough to eschew the contest for the control of the sea lanes through
the eastern Mediterranean, leaving them to Egypt and Phoenicia. It con-
centrated its attention upon the only and chief trade outlet for which it did
not have to struggle with powers immeasurably superior to it, namely upon
Arabia. With its physical nearness and its deep, if at times unconscious
cultural connection with Palestine, Arabia was always for Israel "not
merely a back door but a front portal." The rich routes of commerce coming
from Arabia led northward to Damascus, westward to Gaza and Egypt,
and eastward via Dumah and Teima to the Euphrates and the Persian Gulf.
The nation that sat astride the trade-routes to and from Arabia commanded
the avenues of wealth and power. The wealth of the Edomites and the rapid
rise of the Nabataeans who succeeded them may be partially explained by
their control of these trade routes. The prosperous periods in the history
of the United Kingdom and then of Judah have a direct relationship to the
periods during which they controlled the Arabah and a port on the Red Sea.

It is probable that David carried on the exploitation of the mines in the
Wadi Arabah after he had subjugated and enslaved the Edomites.[5] The
pottery which was used there, however, during this and all the remaining
parts of the Iron Age continued to be Edomite, just as Nabataean pottery
continued to be used after the Romans had occupied the Nabataean sites
in it. Neither David nor any of his successors, who gained control of the
Wadi Arabah and its mines at various times, made any attempt to introduce
other types of pottery than those made by the Edomites, who were probably
compelled to work for them. The exploitation of the mines was undoubtedly
intensified during the reign of Solomon. Indeed, it may be said that he was
the first one who placed the mining industry in the Wadi Arabah upon a
really national scale. Solomon, to be sure, had to contend with guerilla
warfare waged against him by Hadad, who had returned to Edom from
Egypt whither he had fled from David when the latter conquered Edom.[6]

[5] II Samuel 8, 13-15; I Kings 11, 15-16.   [6] I Kings 11, 17-19. 25.

There was a remarkable economic development in Israel during the reign of Solomon, who established himself as the great middleman for the overland trade between Egypt and the Hittite and Aramaean empires,[7] and who also trafficked on a large scale with Arabia.[8] In addition to being a famous sage and a strong-handed, wise ruler, Solomon was in the literal sense of the word a horse-dealer. We read in I Kings 10, 28-29:

And Solomon had horses brought out of Egypt, the king's traders receiving them at a price. A chariot could be imported from Egypt for six hundred and fifty shekels of silver, and a horse for a hundred and fifty. Thus, through their means, was trade carried on with all the kings of the Hittites and the kings of the Aramaeans.

Solomon's mines added great wealth to his growing riches. Quantities of copper must have been used in the construction of the temple and the palace in Jerusalem, but most of it must have served as Solomon's main export and as his merchants' main stock in trade. His Tarshish ships, built and manned with the help of the Phoenicians, sailed from Ezion-geber laden with copper and brought back in exchange gold and other valuable goods, either obtainable in Arabia or trans-shipped there from Africa and India. We read in I Kings 9, 27-28:

And Hiram sent in the navy (of Solomon) his servants, shipmen versed in the sea, together with the servants of Solomon. They came to Ophir and fetched from there four hundred and twenty talents of gold, which they brought to King Solomon.

Solomon's caravans must have penetrated far into Arabia. His ships plied the waters of the Red Sea. In both ventures he was in all probability doing business with, and at the same time competing with, the interests of the famous Queen of Sheba. When one realizes what a terrifically hard journey it must have been for this fair ruler of a rich part of southern Arabia, to come by camel a distance of some 1200 miles or more on her famous trip to Jerusalem to see Solomon, it is hard to believe that she undertook the long and arduous journey merely to bask in the brilliance of the king of Jerusalem. One suspects that this was a trip in which pleasure was mixed with business, and that the Queen of Sheba came to see Solomon partly at least to delimit spheres of interest, and to arrange trade-treaties regulating the equitable exchange of the products of Arabia for the goods of Palestine and particularly the copper of the Wadi Arabah. We read in I Kings 10, 1. 2. 10:

[7] I Kings 10, 1. 2. 14-15. 27; Ezekiel 27, 22.
[8] I Kings 9, 10.

Now when the Queen of Sheba heard of the fame of Solomon, . . . she came to Jerusalem with a very great retinue, with camels bearing spices and very much gold and precious stones. As soon as she came to Solomon, she told him all that was in her heart. Solomon answered all her questions. . . . Then she gave the king one hundred and twenty talents of gold and a very great quantity of spices and precious stones. . . .

The conversations between the two monarchs evidently were mutually satisfactory and reached a successful conclusion because we are told in I Kings 10, 13:

King Solomon gave to the Queen of Sheba all that it pleased her to ask, besides that which he gave to her according to his royal bounty.

After Solomon's death the Red Sea traffic seems to have languished, and Solomon's fleet to have disappeared. When we next hear of Edom, it was ruled by Jehoshaphat through a deputy governor.[9] One may assume therefore that Judah had retained control over Edom from the time of Solomon on and continued to exploit the mines in the Wadi Arabah, although perhaps in a much more limited fashion. Internal peace having been established between Israel and Judah, signalized by the marriage of Jehoshaphat's son, Joram, and Athaliah, daughter of Ahab,[10] Jehoshaphat attempted to reenter the Red Sea trade in which Solomon had so successfully engaged. He accordingly had a number of Tarshish ships built to sail to Ophir to trade copper, we may assume, for the products of Arabia. Unfortunately, however, the ships were broken on the rocks near Ezion-geber,[11] in which wise Solomon's fleet also may finally have been accounted for. Ahaziah, Ahab's son and successor for a brief period, offered then to cooperate in the Red Sea enterprise, but Jehoshaphat refused and the venture was abandoned.[12] It was probably towards the end of his reign that the Edomites made a raid against Engedi.[13] During the reign of his son, Joram, Edom revolted, set up a king in place of the former Judaean deputy,[14] and probably regained control of the Wadi Arabah.

For about a century Judah was unable to push forward again into Edom, which during this period evidently worked the mines in the Wadi Arabah itself. It was, however, not long to enjoy its independence. Amaziah of Judah waged successful war against it, capturing Sela, whose name he changed to Joktheel.[15] His capable son, Uzziah, completed the conquest of Edom begun by his father, it being recorded that he recovered Elath

[9] I Kings 22, 48.
[10] I Kings 22, 45; II Kings 8, 18.
[11] I Kings 22, 49.
[12] I Kings 22, 48-50.
[13] II Chron. 20, 1 ff.
[14] II Kings 8, 20-22.
[15] II Kings 14, 7; II Chron. 25, 11. 12.

from Edom.[16] Elath, as we shall see, was formerly Ezion-geber. Thus he acquired once again access to the trade of the Red Sea and Arabia, using probably as an article of exchange the copper he obtained from the mines in the Wadi Arabah. The marked upswing in the fortunes of Judah during his long reign [17] may be attributed in large part to the wealth obtained from the possession of the Wadi Arabah. Edom then remained subject to Judah till the time of Ahaz, when it regained possession of Elath.[18] After that Judah was never again strong enough to dispute Edom's control over the Wadi Arabah, which Edom itself became progressively less able to hold and exploit. Elath continued to be occupied by the Edomites till the downfall of their kingdom in the 6th century B. C.

In addition to the new information gained from the discoveries in the Wadi Arabah with regard to the ancient history of Palestine and Transjordan, the finds there have verified in a remarkable fashion a particular passage in the Bible whose vagueness had previously troubled scholars, and indeed whose validity had at times been questioned. In the famous description of the Promised Land contained in the exhortation of Moses to his people, we read in Deuteronomy 8, 7-9:

For the Lord thy God bringeth thee into a good land, a land of brooks of water, of fountains and depths that spring out of valleys and hills; a land of wheat and barley, and vines, and figs, and pomegranates; a land of olive oil and honey; a land wherein thou shalt eat bread without scarceness, lacking nothing; *whose stones are iron, and out of whose hills thou canst dig copper.*

It is the last part of the description in which we are particularly interested. It cannot but be meant to apply to the Wadi Arabah, with its rich copper and iron deposits.

X

The mineral deposits in the Wadi Arabah have been far from exhausted. On the contrary, it seems that they have hardly been scratched despite the intensive mining of the ores carried on there particularly during the Iron Age. But it would require considerable initial investment to exploit the ore deposits there today. Roadways would have to be built, water mains laid, refineries erected, settlements established for laborers who would have to be imported, and a short working season of a few months of the year reckoned with, during the late winter and early spring, because of the prohibitive heat during the rest of the year. Whether or not, in view of all these factors and the world prices for copper obtainable in huge quantities elsewhere, the exploitation of the mineral deposits in the Wadi Arabah would

[16] II Chron. 26, 1. 2; II Kings 14, 22.
[17] II Chron. 26, 1-14.   [18] II Kings 16, 6.

be feasible in modern times is a question beyond the competence of the archaeologist. In conclusion of this chapter, it may be of interest to add the results of the chemical analysis of some slag and ore specimens from the Wadi Arabah.

Eight examples were investigated mineralogically and in addition were subjected to chemical analysis either for copper by a volumetric iodine method, or for iron by a volumetric permanganate method, or both, with the following results:

a. Near Qa'ir, two distinct samples.
1. Quartzite, stained with iron.
2. Haematite: 58.7% iron or 83.9% haematite. Most of the residue was silica.

b. Khirbet es-Sabrah.
Haematite: 63.2% iron or 90.4% haematite. Most of the residue was silica.

c. Near Ras es-Sabrah.
Reniform haematite: 58.4% iron or 83.7% haematite; silica residue.

d. Khirbet es-Sabrah slag.
2.73% iron. A trace of copper was indicated by a-benxoin-monoxime.

e. Mene'iyeh.
1. Quartzite.
2. Slag. Qualitative test: iron in large amount.
3. Quartz, stained with malachite or chrysocolla, and attached to quartz mixed with haematite. Since the pieces contain varying proportions of these two components, chemical analysis will also vary. A fairly representative sample contained 13.5% iron and 10.3% copper.

f. Khirbet Nahas.
Sandstone (quartz and kaolin) stained with chalcocite; 7.36% copper.

g. Umm el-Amad.
A composite specimen consisting of:
1. quartz stained with malachite, with
2. black particles which give a good test for manganese and are probably pyrolusite. The specimen contains 0.6% iron and 0.8% copper.

h. Mrashrash.
Slag. This is much harder than the other samples. Systematic qualitative analysis indicates the presence of much silica, much iron, a moderate amount of copper (present in the green stains), and small amounts of aluminum and calcium.

The structure of some of the slags indicates that they were not smelted sufficiently to flow easily, and it is therefore probable that the ore produced reached only a pasty state and was then worked by hand to squeeze out part of the slag contained in it, and yielded an impure wrought iron or an impure copper, as the case may be.

JOHN C. WEAVER,
University of Cincinnati.

Chapter IV

EZION-GEBER: SOLOMON'S SEAPORT

I

King Solomon made a fleet of ships in Ezion-geber, which is beside
Eloth on the shore of the Red Sea in the land of Edom. . . . Once in
three years the fleet came in bringing gold, silver, ivory, apes, peacocks
. . . a very great amount of red sandalwood and precious stones
(I Kings 9: 26; 10: 22, 11.)

Ezion-geber has always been a romantic name to students of ancient
history, but little more. It figured in Biblical accounts before the time of
Solomon as a resting place of the Israelites for a short time during the
years of their wanderings in the wilderness. It is mentioned also as being
the seaport of one of his successors, Jehoshaphat, whose newly built fleet
foundered on the rocks before it could undertake its first voyage. For
almost three thousand years, however, all memory of its location had disappeared from the minds of man, as if it had been little more than a candle-
flame that had flickered fitfully in the night and then been blown out.

The Biblical description of the location of Ezion-geber is sufficient to
give an approximate idea of its whereabouts. In one passage we are told
that the Israelites left Ezion-geber behind when they trekked through the
Arabah on their way to Moab and to the promised land.[1] The Wadi
Arabah, we may repeat, is the great rift which extends between the southern
end of the Dead Sea and the Gulf of Aqabah, and has retained its ancient
name down to this very day. The Gulf of Aqabah is the modern name of
the northeastern tongue of the Red Sea, or the Yam Suf as it is called in
the Hebrew Bible. Somewhere, then, near the southern end of the Wadi
Arabah, facing the Gulf of Aqabah, was located the port of Ezion-geber,
which subsequently became known as Elath.

There were many different theories as to the exact spot of the original
site. Commonly accepted was the notion that the Red Sea had retreated,
during the course of three thousand years, for a distance varying between
twenty-five and thirty-five kilometers, and therefore that Ezion-geber was
to be found nowhere near the present seashore. Scholars paid serious
attention to the story of an imaginative guide who was determined to
furnish his charges with an interesting account upon which they could

---

[1] Deuteronomy 2, 8.

buttress their preconceived notions, failing factual information. Thus, on most of the maps of ancient Palestine, it will be seen that Ezion-geber is located at the head of a supposedly dried-up section of the Gulf of Aqabah, at a distance which is more than an ordinary day's camel ride from the present shore-line.

The story was told that the Gulf of Aqabah once extended as far north as a place called Mene'iyeh, which is about thirty-three kilometers from the present shore-line. At Mene'iyeh, so the tale ran, was an ancient seaport,

Fig. 42.   Direction post at Mrashrash.

whose inhabitants possessed many ships.   Unfortunately, they offended Allah, who caused a long torrential downpour of rain to descend upon the city, with the result that it was completely flooded and destroyed.   Furthermore, great quantities of earth and huge boulders were washed down from the neighboring hills, so choking up the bed of the Gulf that its waters were forced to retreat to their present position.   This fairy story found favor in the eyes of its hearers, and, on the basis of it, maps were marked with an impossible location for Ezion-geber, situated high and dry in the Wadi Arabah, and far from the harbor where once Solomon's ships were actually anchored.   There is some truth to the story that the Gulf of Aqabah has retreated from the ancient shore-line during the course of three thousand years, but the retreat measures some five hundred meters, and not twenty-five thousand or more. (See frontispiece.)

As a result of the discovery of the extensive mining and smelting sites in the Wadi Arabah dating to the time of Solomon, it was possible several years ago to designate Solomon as a great copper king, and by far the most famous of them all. It was known then too that the site of Ezion-geber must be sought somewhere on or very near the present shore-line of the Gulf of Aqabah, because, first of all, as we have seen, one of the mining sites belonging to the period of Solomon had been discovered directly over-

Fig. 43.   Tell Kheleifeh looking .north-northwest.

looking the Gulf.   Secondly, the presence nearby of the ancient site of the originally Nabataean city of Aila, which was occupied practically continuously from the 3rd century B. C. down to the mediaeval Arabic period, and which is located near the northeast shore of the head of the Gulf of Aqabah, precluded the possibility that the north shore-line of the gulf had been radically changed either between the 6th and 3rd centuries B. C. or in the centuries intervening between the mediaeval Arabic period and our day. It remained for a German explorer, named Fritz Frank, to discover an insignificant looking mound, Tell Kheleifeh (Fig. 43), which is situated. above five hundred meters from the shore and is about half way between the eastern and western ends of the head of the gulf.   He found large quantities of pottery fragments on the surface of the mound, which he judged to be old. When the expedition of the American School of Oriental Research at Jerusalem was able to examine the pottery on the site, it was seen immediately that it was the same as the pottery at the mining sites in the rest of the Wadi Arabah to the north, and that the main period of occupation of Tell Kheleifeh must be assigned to and after the time of King Solomon. The American School expedition was thus able to concur in the suggestion of Frank that Tell Kheleifeh should be identified with Ezion-geber.

At last the long-sought-for site had been found, approximately near the location where one would logically imagine it to have been. Soundings were undertaken to determine the approximate outer depth of the debris and the extent of the ruins of the buried city. We learned that the shifting sands blown out of the Wadi Arabah had covered much of the area of the ruined port, and that extensive excavations would have to be undertaken before it could be uncovered and some of its secrets revealed. The American School, with the assistance of a grant from the American Philosophical Society, undertook the excavations there in March, 1938, and finished its first campaign in May of that year. During April and May, 1939, a second season's excavations were carried out, again financed largely by a generous grant from the American Philosophical Society.[2]

The location of Ezion-geber was conditioned by a number of factors. At first glance, one wonders what induced the original builders to choose the particular site they did, because it is about the most uninviting one along the entire shore of the northern end of the Gulf of Aqabah. Situated in the bottom of a curve banked on the east side by the hills of Edom, which continue into Arabia, and on the west side by the hills of Palestine, which continue into Sinai, it is open to the full fury of the winds and sandstorms from the north, that blow along the center of the Wadi Arabah as if forced through a wind tunnel.

It is not difficult to understand why the port could not have been built farther to the west. From Mrashrash, at the northwestern end of the Gulf, to the site of Ezion-geber, there is no sweet water obtainable for drinking purposes in a distance of some three and a half kilometers. The police stationed at Mrashrash send all the way to Aqabah, at the northeastern end of the Gulf, about seven kilometers, for their drinking water. The point where the sweet-water wells begin is marked almost exactly by the location of the ruins of Ezion-geber. From there eastwards there is a continuous

---

[2] A third campaign, assisted by the Smithsonian Institution, is in progress as this book goes to press.—ED.

line of such wells, increasing in number the closer one gets to Aqabah, and marked by a correspondingly increasing number of date-palm trees between the two points.

While one realizes, then, why the early builders of Ezion-geber could not very well have built farther to the west, one wonders at first why they did not build farther to the east, nearer to the site of the modern mud-brick village of Aqabah. There is more water and more protection there from the winds and the sandstorms of the Wadi Arabah. The actual excavations were to reveal that the founders of the city had acted wisely. The sand-storms frequently made our work impossible, and at times blotted out vision of the Gulf at a distance of a hundred meters. By the simple process of walking less than a kilometer to the east or west of the site, it was possible to escape the sandstorms; and, looking back, one could see great clouds of sand hovering over the mound and moving directly in front of it towards the sea, calling to mind the Biblical description of the pillar of cloud by day and the pillar of fire by night. The strong winds which blow steadily from the north were evidently a feature so desirable to the architects of Ezion-geber that they built the city directly in their path.

II

The excavations were begun at the northwest end of the mound for various reasons, not the least of them being consideration for the direction of the winds. It was found that all the houses were made of mud-brick. A large building with ten rooms, which occupied the entire northwest corner of the mound, was opened up. It soon became evident that this was not an ordinary large building or palace, but a completely novel type of structure, the like of which had not previously been discovered in the entire ancient Near East. The walls of the rooms were pierced with two rows of flues, and the main walls were interconnected by a system of air-channels inside the walls, into which the upper rows of flues opened. The lower rows completely pierced the thickness of the walls between the rooms. The originally unfired yellowish mud-bricks had been baked, by the heat of the fires in the rooms, to the consistency of kiln-fired bricks. Masses of hard baked clay-debris, on which pottery crucibles had been placed, completed the picture. It became evident that the building was an elaborate smelter or refinery, where previously " roasted " ores were worked up into ingots of purer metal. It was obvious, both from the sulphuric discoloration of the walls and from the fragments of raw ore and numerous finished articles discovered, that the refinery at Ezion-geber was devoted mainly to copper, of which, as we have seen, great quantities abound in the immediate vicinity and along most of the length of the Wadi Arabah, and in adjacent Sinai. Iron also was treated in this plant (Figs. 44-48).

During the second season of excavations we discovered that the smelter at the northwest corner of the site was not unique at Ezion-geber, but was merely a unit in an elaborate complex of industrial plants of similar nature. They were all devoted to the smelting and refining of copper and iron and the manufacturing of metal articles for home and foreign markets. The entire town, in its first and second periods, was a phenomenal industrial site. A forced draft system for the furnaces was employed, and later abandoned and forgotten, to be re-discovered only in modern times. Ezion-geber was the Pittsburgh of Palestine, in addition to being its most important port. Its rooms were, so to speak, air-conditioned for heat.

The reason, then, why the original builders of Ezion-geber chose the inclement site they did for the location of their city was that they wanted the strong winds blowing from a known direction to furnish the draft for the furnace rooms in the refineries, and enable them to dispense with an expensive and burdensome bellows system. It was a matter of harnessing the elements for industrial purposes. More important to them than much water for fine palm groves, and protection from sandstorms on a location farther to the east, were strong and continuous winds which would enable them to operate the refineries with their intricate system of flues and air-channels.

In addition to the fact that the entire first town of Ezion-geber, which for convenience we shall call Ezion-geber I, represented a carefully integrated industrial complex, the excavations have shown that it was built completely anew on virgin soil, and that it experienced no gradual growth and development but was built at one time, within the space of a year or two, from a preconceived and carefully worked-out plan. Surveyors, architects, and engineers had evidently looked over the north shore of the Gulf of Aqabah in advance with a view to the particular requirements they had in mind. They were industrial scouts, sent out to spy out the land, and they chose a town-site which no builders would have selected in the normal course of events for the founding of a settlement. They needed, as we have seen, strong and continuous winds, coming from a known direction to provide drafts for furnaces; they needed also sweet water to drink, a central point commanding strategic commercial and military cross-roads, and access to the sea. Great quantities of copper and iron were present in the Wadi Arabah, and provided the most important impetus for the building of the first town on the site known to-day as Tell Kheleifeh (Fig. 49).

Fig. 44. Panorama of the excavations at Tell Kheleifeh.

Fig. 45. Tell Kheleifeh. Smelting and refining plant, showing flues in walls.

The town site chosen, intricate plans for the establishing of a very complicated factory complex must have been drawn up. A great deal of specialized technical skill was necessary. Thick and high walls of sun-dried bricks had to be erected, with flues and air-channels in them, and with allowances made for the weight of the wall above them. The angle of the buildings had carefully to be chosen to get the full benefit of the winds from the north. Bricks had to be made by the thousands, and laid by expert brick-layers. In no period in the history of the subsequent towns,

Fig. 46. Tell Kheleifeh. Outer south wall of the refinery, showing two rows of flues.

each built on top of the ruins of the previous one, were bricks as excellently made and skillfully laid as during the first period. Certainly not in the poor little town of Aqabah several miles to the east, which in modern times has superseded Ezion-geber. All the bricks were laid in complicated systems of headers and stretchers, with the corners of the walls well bonded together. One reads today of new towns, planned in advance, and springing up as if by magic on previously bare soil with the aid of modern transportation facilities and mechanical equipment. Ezion-geber, however, still remote from civilized points today, was a long and difficult journey from them in ancient times. It took the writer thirteen days on camel back, several

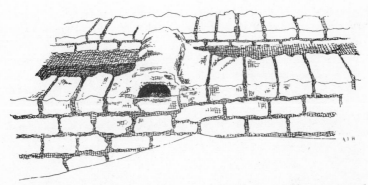

Fig. 47. Tell Kheleifeh. East wall of refinery, showing one of the transverse flues through which air flowed into a channel running lengthwise inside of the wall.

Fig. 48. Flues in the south wall of furnace room 1 in the refinery at Tell Kheleifeh.

8

years ago, to travel from the south end of the Dead Sea, which is already camparatively far from Jerusalem, to the north shore of the Gulf of Aqabah. It took a great deal of business ability, as well as architectural, engineering,

Fig. 49. A street of Ezion-geber looking west.

and metallurgical skill to construct the factory town and seaport of Ezion-geber, and to keep the production-line going.

One can easily visualize the conditions existing about three millennia ago, when the idea of building this place was first conceived and then brilliantly translated into reality. Thousands of laborers had to be assembled, housed, fed, and protected at the chosen building site. As a matter of fact, most of them were probably slaves, who had to be guarded and goaded to work. Skilled technicians of all kinds had to be recruited. Great caravans had to be collected to transport materials and food. An effective business organization had to be called into existence to regulate the profitable flow of raw materials and finished or semi-finished products. There was, so far as we know, only one man who possessed the strength, wealth and wisdom capable of initiating and carrying out such a highly complex and specialized undertaking. He was King Solomon. He alone in his day had the ability, the vision, and the power to establish an important industrial center and sea-port such a comparatively long distance from the capital city of Jerusalem

The wise ruler of Israel was a copper king, a shipping magnate, a merchant prince, and a great builder. Through his manifold activities, he became at once the blessing and the curse of his country. With increased power and wealth came a centralization of authority and a ruthless dictatorship which ignored the democratic traditions of his own people. There resulted a counter-development of forces of reaction and revolt, which were immediately after Solomon's death to rend his kingdom asunder. During his lifetime, however, Solomon reigned supreme. The evil he did lived after him. His far-flung net of activities extended from Egypt to Phoenicia, and from Arabia to Syria. Ezion-geber represents one of his greatest, if indeed up to the present time his least known accomplishments.

III

Further proof is required that Ezion-geber I was built by Solomon's men. This can now be furnished through archaeological evidence. Among the most important discoveries at Tell Kheleifeh were those of the outer fortification wall and the gateway of Ezion-geber I. Their foundations rested on virgin soil. The fortification wall had been built so well and so regularly that it was possible, after parts of it had been exposed, to plot out its course and determine its lines for the most part by at first merely trenching at intervals along its length. At the presently preserved top of the wall, which is almost flush with the level of the desert, the wall is from about 2.50 to 3 meters thick. Its foundation courses go down below the soil about a meter. In many places the lowest foundation course rests on a natural, hard clay stratum; in other instances on sand. As the wall goes downward, it widens out, sometimes in three successive steps of two rows of bricks each,

EMORY AND HENRY LIBRARY,

71378

(Fig. 50), so that in some places the wall is almost 4 meters thick at
its base. The wall is built of sun-dried bricks, like the rest of the site,
laid carefully in alternate rows of headers and stretchers, and must easily

Fig. 50.   Foundation levels of outer fortification wall of Ezion-geber.

have been 8 meters high. There are strongly marked offsets along the sides
of the walls and particularly at the corners.

The main gateway leading into the town was found near the southwest
corner of the wall, on the south side, facing the sea. There were three
gates in this entrance way, built at intervals one behind the other, the first
two of which opened respectively into separate sets of guard-rooms behind

each gate, with one room on each side of the entrance (Fig. 51). Thus if
the first gate were broken down, the enemy would still have to pass the
two rectangular guardrooms facing each other on the opposite sides of the
entrance (Fig. 52); and so too if the second gate were broken down. The
third gate opened into the main street of the town, which made a sharp
right-angled turn to the east. To the west and north, the third gate seems
also to have led into a large open square, where the market-place will
undoubtedly be found, and in a section of which the camels of visiting
caravans may have been kept at night. The amazing thing about Ezion-
geber I is that a place of such comparatively small size should be surrounded by such a tremendously strong outer fortification wall, with
its three-doored gateway. The entire site, walls and all, covers an area
no larger than approximately an acre and a half, about large enough for
a villa with a good sized garden in a modern suburb.

The three-doored gateway of Ezion-geber I is directly related to the
south gate of the inner town of Carchemish on the Euphrates, as well as
to the west gate of the outer town of Carchemish. New evidence from
Megiddo has shown that the gateway which was regarded by Guy as belonging to Stratum IV at Megiddo, and which he compared with the south
gate at Carchemish, may actually belong to Stratum III, dated 780-650 B. C.
This gateway is closely related in plan to that of Ezion-geber I. We
consider it likely that when the nature of the Solomonic gateway at Megiddo
has been definitely established, it will be shown to be almost, if not completely identical with the gateway of Ezion-geber I. Guy's original date
of the Solomonic period for Stratum IV at Megiddo, aside from the gateway, still stands. Guy's remarks with regard to Stratum IV at Megiddo
are worth quoting, because of their direct bearing upon the dating of
Ezion-geber I:

So far, we have found nothing archaeologically inconsistent with an immediately
post-Philistine date for Stratum IV. As to the buildings, we get well-planned structures, with much dressed stone well laid and well bonded by evidently skilled workmen. We have the use of datum lines by masons, *and proof that weights were
carefully allowed for by the architects before building was begun. And we get all
those things occurring suddenly, in a city apparently planned and built as a whole*
[italics are mine], with its walls, its gate[?], its streets, and a remarkable number
of stables strangely similar to buildings discovered elsewhere which have been
independently dated to the ninth or tenth century B. C.

Guy's identification of the builder of Stratum IV at Megiddo with
Solomon has long been generally accepted. We have already seen that
Ezion-geber I, like Stratum IV at Megiddo, was planned in advance, and
built with considerable architectural and engineering skill at one time as

Fig. 51. Ezion-geber. Looking north at main gateway in south wall
near southwest corner.

Fig. 52. General view from southwest. First guard-room on east side of
gateway, behind the entrance, in Ezion-geber I. The wall which
blocked the entrance to the guard-room in Ezion-geber II
was removed during the excavations.

an integrated whole. This fact, in addition to other independent archaeological evidence, makes it seem probable that the builder of Ezion-geber I
was none other than the builder of Stratum IV at Megiddo and of numerous
other sites throughout the length and breadth of Palestine, namely King

Fig. 53. Looking south through gateway of Ezion-geber toward the Gulf of Aqabah.

Solomon. Lankester Harding has called my attention to the fact, and
graciously given me permission to mention it, that there is a gateway at
Lachish in southwestern Palestine, assigned by the excavators to the 10th
century B. C, and attributed to Solomon, which is almost exactly the same
as the gateway at Ezion-geber I (Fig. 53) and those at Carchemish.

The likelihood, therefore, that there was no one besides King Solomon in greater Palestine during the latter part of the 10th century B. C., who possessed the energy and the ability and power and wealth to build such a site as Ezion-geber I, seems to become a certainty through the clear archaeological evidence at our disposal. We find it significant that at the very end of the account in I Kings 9 of Solomon's manifold building activities throughout Palestine, there is narrated in some detail the story of the construction of a fleet of ships for him at Ezion-geber, which, manned by Phoenician sailors, sailed to Ophir for gold. For some reason or other, the author of this account failed to mention the fact that Solomon exported ingots of copper and iron and finished metal objects on these ships for the gold and other products obtainable in Ophir; and also failed to state that in all probability at the same time as the ships were being constructed, the port-city and industrial town of Ezion-geber I was also being built.

Inasmuch as the Ezion-geber of Solomon was found to rest on virgin soil, with no traces whatsoever of earlier remains, it becomes necessary to conclude that this is not the Ezion-geber which the Israelites saw when they emerged from the Wilderness of Sinai after the sojourn there lasting forty years. They saw probably a tiny, straggling settlement, with a few mud-brick huts and scraggly palms, farther to the east, where the drinking water is less saline and the sandstorms do not occur. All traces of this earlier site have disappeared, only its name surviving in the bustling town of Ezion-geber I, whose finer residential suburb must also, however, have been farther east, near the site of the modern village of Aqabah.

IV

After the destruction by fire of Ezion-geber I, it was rebuilt in the subsequent period and functioned again as an industrial town of much the same nature as its predecessor. Changes were made in the outer fortifications. A secondary wall was placed outside the former main wall of the previous city, and the gateway was altered. The main changes in the gateway, in addition to the fact that the floor-level was raised, are that the entrances to the two pairs of guard-rooms were blocked up, creating thus four small, squarish rooms behind the passageway, and an additional mud-brick pillar was put on each side of the third gateway, narrowing the passageway. In other words, the general scheme of the gateway of Ezion-geber I with three doors was adhered to, but the guard-rooms were transformed into casemates.

The Solomonic city at Megiddo was destroyed by the Egyptian king Shishak (954-924 B. C.). It does not necessarily follow that Ezion-geber I was destroyed at the same time as Stratum IV at Megiddo, although the possibility must be considered. Professor Albright has called the writer's attention to the fact that in Shishak's list of conquered Asiatic cities, found at Karnak in Egypt, a large section of the names must be Edomite, as pointed out independently by himself and Noth. The general industrial, commercial, and strategic importance of the Wadi Arabah, with its rich mines, and of Ezion-geber, made them a fine prize for invaders. It is interesting in this connection that Albright proposes to explain *ngb* in the Shishak list as Hebrew *nqb*, "tunnel, shaft, mine." Noth also has marshalled considerable evidence indicating that Shishak's campaign extended rather far east of the south side of Palestine, and may in this area have been directed toward the Wadi Arabah. In view of these considerations, and of general and specific archaeological data which cannot be further detailed here, we think it likely that Ezion-geber I was destroyed by Shishak's forces during the same campaign which resulted in the destruction of many towns in Palestine, including Megiddo, shortly after Solomon's death.

When fire radically destroyed the second settlement, there was built over it a third one. In its later history, the site of Ezion-geber was called Elath or Eloth. The third city, in which two periods can be distinguished, was constructed on entirely new lines without regard for the walls or foundations of the preceding settlements, and it is, on the whole, the best preserved one. Many of its walls still stand almost to their original height, and in a number of instances the houses could be completely reconstructed on paper. In a report on the excavations at Hureidha in the Hadhramaut in South Arabia, Miss Caton-Thompson has described one of the homesteads unearthed there. The excavations disclosed a mud-brick building, formerly white-washed, fitted with mud-brick benches. Logs of wood reinforced the door-treads. The ceiling had been constructed, in the fashion still practiced in the region, of twigs laid in parallel bundles across the rafters and over-daubed with mud. This description fits almost exactly the houses in Ezion-geber: Elath at an earlier date (Fig. 54), and modern Arabic mud-brick houses near there today (Fig. 55).

During the first season of excavations we discovered on the level of the third city the fragments of a large jar, on two of whose pieces were incised the first ancient South Arabic letters ever discovered in a controlled excavation. These letters belong to the Minaean script. The Minaeans are reported by Pliny to be the oldest known commercial people in South

Fig. 54. Mud-brick house in Ezion-geber, almost intact except for flat roof; in foreground thieves' hole, patched.

Fig. 55. Modern mud-brick house near Ezion-geber, its wall not bonded together as in the case of its ancient prototype.

Arabia, controlling the Incense Route, and monopolizing the trade in myrrh and frankincense. It has been possible since the discovery of these fragments to put them together, and thus to restore most of the shape of the jar, which may well have been the container of precious products from as far away as South Arabia (Fig. 56). It was perhaps in similar jars

Fig. 56. A restored jar with South Arabian inscription
from Tell Kheleifeh.

that the Queen of Sheba brought some of her valuable presents to King Solomon. It may have belonged to a Minaean trade representative living in Elath.

In an article on Arabia Miss Caton-Thompson wrote: "And so the Eziongeber sherd—dating from a century or two after Solomon—with its lettered hall-mark of South Arabian origin, may be a rarity which not all the

excavations to come will convert into a commonplace of finds." During
the second season of excavations at Tell Kheleifeh, yet another ancient
Arabic inscription was found on a large jar, in the same level as the one
previously discovered. It may be an owner's mark. The discovery of this
additional inscription emphasizes again the intimate commercial relationship between Ezion-geber: Elath and Arabia, and underlines anew the
importance of the former as a trade-center and seaport, as well as an important industrial site. Miss Caton-Thompson and her colleagues have
recently discovered South Arabian inscriptions during the excavations of
the temple at Hureidha, apparently first built in the 4th century B. C.
They are similar in type to the Minaean characters found incised on the
jar at Tell Kheleifeh. The Hureidha inscriptions thus again furnish an
approximate date, less definite to be sure than that obtained from the excavations at Tell Kheleifeh, upon which the history of the South Arabian
type of ancient Arabian writing can be pegged. The distance between
Ezion-geber and Hureidha is approximately 1200 miles, and about four
centuries intervene between the South Arabian inscriptions found at the
two sites. It begins to appear, however, that both places were set in one
cultural pattern, and that Arabia continued into what is today called Transjordan, and thus in ancient times almost literally abutted the territory of
Israel. To this day, for instance, the "skyscraper" houses of southern
Arabia, described in recent books such as Freya Stark's *Southern Gates of
Arabia,* linger on in ruined form as far north as Ma'an in southern Transjordan. The site at the southern end of the great Spice Route, definitely
contemporary with Ezion-geber: Elath, is bound sooner or later to be found.

In addition to the trade by sea and land with Arabia, much evidence
was discovered of trade with Egypt and Sinai. There were found, particularly in the third town built on the site, counting from the bottom up,
such varied objects coming from Sinai and Egypt as carnelian, agate,
amethyst and crystal beads, cartouche-like seal impressions, a tiny faience
amulet head of the god Bes, a small Egyptian amulet of a cat, fragments
of alabaster cups and plates and buttons, and a part of a scaraboid bead.
The cat amulet (Fig. 57) was characteristic of the cult of the goddess
Bast, whose temple was at Bubastis in Egypt, which was also the seat of
the XXIInd dynasty. The founder of that dynasty was Sheshonk I
(Shishak), mentioned above.

Stamped impressions were found on pottery, revealing both Syrian and
Arabian influence. Various designs were found incised on some of the
pottery fragments, one of which looked like a "Byzantine" cross, another
of which resembled the "Star of David," and a third one which was like

Fig. 57. Egyptian Bubastite cat amulet, much enlarged,
indicative of traffic with Pharaonic Egypt.

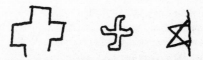

Fig. 58. Familiar modern symbols used by potters at Ezion-geber (Elath).

a swastika—in this instance a "non-Aryan" swastika (Fig. 58). Stamped jar handles were discovered bearing the legend in ancient Edomite-Phoenician-Hebrew characters *belonging to Qws'nl the servant of the king* (Fig. 59). A small jug was found with a late Edomite inscription which may perhaps be read as *belonging to Am(zrn)* (Fig. 60).

Of much interest were numerous large copper and iron nails (the copper ones being a mixture of iron and copper), found in the third and fourth town. These nails, spikes really, are usually about six inches long. It seems reasonable to believe that they were used in the construction of boats, an important activity of the industrial life of each of the towns built on the site. Pitch was found, used probably, at least partially, for caulking the boats. Furthermore, in several rooms of the two uppermost towns were found numerous fragments of ropes of all sizes, some of them so large and thick that they could only have been used for ship ropes. Some of the smaller ropes were made of twisted palm branches, much as they are in Aqabah today. The larger three-coil ropes were made of hundreds of fibre threads taken from the bark of the palm tree, twisted into large cords and coils and then twisted into a thick, heavy rope. The art of making this type of rope is no longer known in the modern village of Aqabah. Oak planks from timber cut in the forests of the hills of Edom furnished the basic material for the building of the boats, even as these forests furnished the fuel, converted into charcoal, for firing the smelting furnaces in the Wadi Arabah and at Ezion-geber, as we have pointed out. Phoenician craftsmen constructed the boats in all probability, and Phoenician sailors manned them. They gave them the name by which the boats sailing from Phoenicia to Tarshish were known, namely, Tarshish boats. Besides copper and iron nails, other metal objects were found, including fish-hooks, lance- and spear-heads, daggers, fragments of copper dishes, and fibulae, the safety pin of the Iron Age. Pottery, much of it peculiar to this site, beads, cloth, and baskets were also manufactured.

V

When the third town, which had two periods of occupation, was destroyed by fire, a fourth town was built above it. The foundations of the walls of this fourth town were now between 3.50 and 4 meters above the foundations of the walls of the first town. Whether or not this town was surrounded by an outer fortification wall is impossible to say at present. The likelihood seems to be, to judge from the first two towns, that both of the latter ones were also surrounded by outer fortification walls. There is but little

Fig. 59. Impression of seal of Qws'nl, enlarged about 8 diameters.

Fig. 60. Jug with late Edomite inscription, reading perhaps
belonging to Am(zrn).

of the fourth town left, because it has been weathered away except on the highest part of the mound. Enough of it was unearthed, however, to show that it was a town of a size comparable with that of the preceding one. A new type of brick was used during its construction. This fourth town was also ultimately destroyed by fire. Whatever buildings, if any, may have been constructed subsequently above its ruins, have completely disappeared.

A few centimeters, on the average, below the topmost surface of the mound at its highest level, were found a number of imported Greek sherds, which belong probably to the latest phase of the fourth town. These sherds were pieces of imported red-figured and degenerate black-figured Attic ware, which may be dated to about the middle of the 5th century B. C. They were probably brought from Greece to Gaza or Ascalon, and then taken by the trade-route which led from Ascalon and Gaza to Qurnub, then to Ain Hosb, and thence through the Wadi Arabah directly to Elath, or via Petra to various sites in Transjordan. This is the trade-route which assumed great importance particularly during the Nabataean period, and continued in use through the Byzantine period. These Attic sherds had travelled a long distance from the shores of Greece to the northern shores of the Gulf of Aqabah, and furnish indisputable evidence of the presence of a settlement on Tell Kheleifeh during the first half of the 5th century B. C. It was probably a trading community, whose existence depended in all likelihood upon the great incense and spice traffic, which continued as of old to flow along the route from Arabia to Elath, whence it diverged to Transjordan, Syria, Persia, Palestine, and the Mediterranean countries. It would seem likely now that Attic pottery of the 5th century B. C. should be discovered also in Arabia, because the wares found at Tell Kheleifeh were in all probability transhipped farther south, either because of their own intrinsic value or because they may have been containers of products, such as wines, for instance, which were exchanged for the spices of Arabia. There are no indications of extensive mining and smelting of copper and iron deposits in the Wadi Arabah during the 5th century B. C., which would have yielded the export commodities similar to those available in great quantities to Solomon in exchange for the precious products obtainable from South Arabia.

Belonging to the same period as the Attic sherds, and also found near the top surface of the mound, were several small, broken, Aramaic ostraca. Some of them were written with the same characters as found on the Elephantine papyri and ostraca found in Egypt, and may, like them, be assigned to the 5th century B. C. and later. One was a wine receipt. They are part of the same picture of occupation that is furnished by the Attic sherds.

They also lend a definite basis for the suggestion made above, that products of various kinds, including wine, perhaps even Greek wines, were imported to Elath and then exported to Arabia in exchange for its incense and spices.

With this last settlement the history of Ezion-geber: Elath was concluded. It extended from the 10th to the 5th century B. C., and perhaps even a century later. When the Nabataeans subsequently rose to great power, they also built a trade-center and port on the north shore of the Gulf of Aqabah, but moved it about three kilometers farther to the east, where in Roman times it was known as Aila. The hey-day of Ezion-geber, later to be known as Elath, was during the time of Solomon in the 10th century B. C.

CHAPTER V

EDOM, MOAB, AMMON, AND GILEAD

I

The amazing historical memory reflected in many stories in the Bible which deal with ancient events, reveals itself in one account which is pertinent to our subject, and to which we have already alluded. It concerns itself with the early Bronze Age civilization of an agricultural and permanent character in Transjordan, which precedes and is separated from the subsequent Iron Age civilization of like character by a gap in time of about 600 years, during which only Bedouins peopled the land. Somehow or other, by word of mouth from father to son in the living tradition of unwritten lore, the accounts of episodes in Transjordan which occurred in or about the Age of Abraham were repeated, until finally caught for long time to come in the written pages of the Bible. We are told in Genesis 14, 5-7 of the Eastern kings led by Chedorlaomer, who conquered all of Transjordan by picking off piecemeal, from Ashtaroth and Ham at its northern end as far as El-paran at its southern end, all the fortified sites which lay in their path, and which apparently made no effort to face the enemy with a united front.

The archaeological facts agree completely with this literary tradition. There was at about ± 1900 B. C. such a thoroughgoing destruction visited upon all the great fortresses and settlements of the land, within the limits we have examined, that the particular civilization they represented never again recovered. The blow it received was so crushing as to be utterly destructive. Its cities were never rebuilt, and much of Transjordan became the camping ground of tent dwellers, who used for containers perishable skins and not enduring pottery. Permanent villages and fortresses were no longer to rise upon the face of the earth in this region till the beginning of the Iron Age.

What manner of civilization was it that flourished so briefly, particularly between the 23rd and the 20th century B. C.? What kind of settlements and houses did its bearers live in? What occupations engaged their time and energy? What traces of their being did they leave behind them? What prevented the entire land of Transjordan from being settled at least as intensively also in the Middle and Late Bronze Ages, i. e. between the end of the 20th and the beginning of the 13th century B. C., as it was in the

114

Hauran and apparently in northern Gilead, and as it was in Western Palestine?

The early Bronze Age settlements were found scattered throughout the length and breadth of the land. As we have already seen, a long line of them existed along the route of the main north-south track through central Transjordan. They were, it will be seen, firmly established farming communities, representative of a highly advanced agricultural civilization. Most of them are to be found in the midst of the fertile plateau lands of Transjordan. Many of these sites have undoubtedly completely disappeared. During all the ages following this early Bronze Age period of settlement and cultivation of the soil in Transjordan, the more fertile lands have been the first to be preempted and employed for agriculture. The older the ancient sites are, therefore, in these particular areas, the less likely it becomes that traces of many of them will have survived throughout the millennia, either because subsequently they have been completely ploughed up and defy detection under fields of grain, or because modern settlements have been built over them, burying under huge piles of debris the scanty remains of the earliest inhabitants. Nevertheless, a considerable number of these 23rd-20th century B. C. sites has been found, both in the midst of areas intensively cultivated today and on their fringes.

On the north slope of the western part of the Wadi Hesa (the River Zered) is a fairly flat and then rising shelf of tilled land, kept in place by ancient terraces, and rising to a natural saddle fixed between two pommels of great, isolated, natural rock-towers. On this saddle were the remains of a large, completely ruined site, which had at one time been surrounded by a strong outer wall. It is called Khirbet Umm Sedeirah (Fig. 61). Large quantities of early Bronze Age sherds were found on the terraces surrounding this site, and also on top of the ruins proper, where, in addition, a few Nabataean sherds were found. Water for the ancient settlement was supplied by the spring called Ain Ghabah, which rises immediately below this site to the southeast.

The presence of this site on the slope of the Wadi Hesa, possible only because of careful terracing laboriously carried out, indicates almost without the necessity of other evidence that in the early part of the Bronze Age southern Moab was intensively occupied by people belonging to an agricultural civilization. Certainly the more fertile areas on top of the plateau would have been the first to have been utilized. Only dire necessity could compel the use of fields for farming which under normal circumstances would not have been turned up by the plough, and the building of terrace walls to protect them. Thus while parts of the fields by Khirbet

9

Umm Sedeirah are cultivated today, most of the fairly extensive walled terraces are no longer used, but are broken and cut with the gashes of neglect. The waters of seasonal rains finding nothing to stem their downward flood tear paths through the once productive fields and leave a barren hillside behind them, with bare ribs of rock protruding from such soil as has not yet been washed down into the *wadi* below. Terracing, soil conservation, water economy, preservation of forests, all of which seem to have been the self-understood rote and rule of the former inhabitants of Transjordan from the earliest agricultural history of the region to and through

Fig. 61. Khirbet Umm Sedeirah, with south slope of Wadi Hesa in background.

the Byzantine period, are, on the whole, no longer known or understood by their successors in the land.

Due north of Khirbet Umm Sedeirah, and well within the area of the fertile plateau land of southern Moab, is another early Bronze Age site called el-Mudowwerah, on a completely isolated hill. The entire hilltop, which has the shape roughly of a great truncated triangle, was once enclosed by a strong outer wall. Parts of it are still visible, particularly along the southwest side. The wall bends and curves in accordance with the lines of the top of the hill, enclosing an area measuring about 300 by 300 by 100 meters. The east slope of the hill is the least precipitous, and there are clear traces of a roadway leading up to the entrance at the southeast corner of the site. The top of the hill is today completely ploughed over and regularly planted to wheat and *dhurah*, as are to a degree the slopes beneath the enclosing wall, which were anciently terraced. Inside this great enclosure, and also on the slopes immediately below its walls, were found large numbers of early Bronze Age sherds. We were not able to establish the source of the water which must have been available to the inhabitants of the site.

Along the north side of the Wadi Mojib we found a number of large early Bronze Age sites. They were built along the edge of the same fertile plateau where during the Iron Age Mesha, king of Moab, erected a number of cities and laid out a roadway. Traces of the first historical settlements along this line can still be clearly seen at Khirbet Aqrabah, Arair, and Lehun. Khirbet Aqrabah furnishes a good example of a site, all traces of which would have completely disappeared were it not for the fragments of pottery which remained despite all the vicissitudes of time. At the point where the new road being built today through central Transjordan, practically on the line used in ancient times, begins the descent down the steep slope of the Wadi Mojib, is the site of Khirbet Aqrabah. Above the point where the road makes its first bend around a prominent outspur, we found large quantities of early Bronze Age sherds. The foreman of the road-gang found a complete, small, flat-bottomed handmade jug, with one loop-handle and wet-smoothed, reddish-buff surface. His men had dug it up while cutting through the hillside at this bend. It can be dated to about the 21st century B. C.

No other complete vessels were found. No visible traces of house- or wall-foundations remained. Even the soil which had obviously once covered the top of the outspur had been swept away by seasonal rains, when the walls which helped hold it in place had been breached and destroyed either by nature or man. Many stones may also have been removed by the successive Nabataean to mediaeval Arabic sites in the neighborhood. Quarrying operations among ancient ruins are going on all over Transjordan today, particularly if they happen to be located near modern and growing settlements. The Transjordan Department of Antiquities is attempting, however, to prevent these depredations.

Somewhat less than 10 kilometers north-northeast of Khirbet Aqrabah, at a point where, coming from the north, the new road through central Transjordan fords the Wadi Wala, is Khirbet Iskander, which turned out to be another 23rd to 20th century B. C. site. It is built on a low mound with its south side reaching to the very edge of the north bank of the Wadi Wala, which at this point has been sliced away straight and steep by the continuously and swiftly flowing stream in the *wadi*. In the days of the Eastern kings it dominated the ford crossing the stream, even as the site of

Rujm Mlehleb, to the west of it, dominated this crossing in the times of the Moabites. The eminence on which Khirbet Iskander is located is cut into two parts by two small *wudyan* which, coming from the north, join the Wadi Wala. The west section is still enclosed with the remnants of a strong wall, and measures about 150 meters square. There are clear foundation remains of houses built against the walls inside the enclosure. The east section is dotted with *menhir*-circles and large standing and fallen *menhirs*, belonging to the contemporary cemetery. In both sections were numerous sherds, dating from the 23rd to the 20th century B.C.

Khirbet Iskander extended at one time apparently on both sides of the Wadi Wala. Just west of the point on the south side of the *wadi*, where the new road crosses the stream and begins the ascent to the south, there stands an imposing limestone monolith, about 3 meters high. Another one, half buried, stands close by it (Fig. 62). The large monolith has a striking resemblance to the ones at the early Bronze Age sites of Ader and el-Megheirat. When one considers in this connection the somewhat smaller, similar stones at the early Bronze Age Lejjun (Fig. 63), and those found by Albright and Kyle at the early Bronze Age site of Bab edh-Dhra overlooking the Dead Sea above Lisan, there seems to be reason to believe that all such standing stones in Transjordan should be assigned to the same period.

In this connection, it may be appropriate to give expression to our belief that many, if indeed not all of the large dolmens which are to be found in Transjordan are to be likewise dated. At el-Megheirat there exists besides the Hajr Mansub a large dolmen field, directly related to it. By indirection, therefore, it also should be assigned to the same period in the early Bronze Age as the Hajr Mansub, and the monoliths at Ader, Khirbet Iskander, and Lejjun. Père de Vaux of the Dominican Ecole Biblique et Archéologique Française in Jerusalem has recently discovered at el-Megheirat a large number of sherds which definitely belong to this period, extending from the 23rd to the 20th century B.C. He has thus, we believe, furnished final proof for the dating of the dolmens in Transjordan to the early Bronze Age.

We visited another dolmen field during the course of our survey of southern Gilead, on one of the hilltops not far from the Wadi Zerqa. It is called Arqub Ibn Hadad, and is close to another place called Rujm Nebi Hadad, where a sherd was found which could unmistakably be assigned to ± 2000 B.C. Nearby was a third site known as Rujm Bint Hadad. At Arqub Ibn Hadad we found a field of apparently eleven dolmens, most of which are now in a more or less ruinous state. They are, we believe, to be assigned to the period, the end of which is represented by the one sherd from

Fig. 62. Menhir at Khirbet Iskander.

Fig. 63. Standing pillars at Lejjun.

Rujm Nebi Hadad. One dolmen at Arqub Ibn Hadad is still fairly intact, and rests upon what was apparently once a circular base. No sherds were found on the site (Fig. 64).

A large dolmen built on a massive circular base was found beside another early Bronze Age site, called el-Qeseir. El-Qeseir is situated on top of a great, completely isolated hill which towers from the west above the Beq'ah, the rich valley south of the Wadi Zerqa, through which the traveller must pass on his way from Suweileh on the Jericho-Amman road to Jerash. The remains of a large outer wall are visible. The walled area measures

Fig. 64. Dolmen at Arqub Ibn Hadad.

approximately 325 by 42 meters. A considerable number of early Bronze Age sherds were found, and also several Byzantine and mediaeval Arabic sherds. Both the south and north ends of the hilltop are higher than the rest of the enclosed area, and to judge from building stones at these points, it seems likely that they were once crowned with watch-towers. Near the base of the east side of the hill is a spring called Ain Khaneizir. The cisterns found at the site were so filled with debris, and almost completely covered with fallen building blocks, that all that can be said about them is that they were cisterns. Our general impression is that these early Bronze Age places depended upon springs or wells or perennial streams for their sources of water. It may be assumed that in addition to the cultivation carried on inside the walled area and on the slopes of the hill, the inhabitants of el-Qeseir cultivated considerable portions of the rich valley of the Beq'ah.

About 9 kilometers north of Amman is another huge, formerly walled, early Bronze Age site called Kom Yajuz, situated on top of a high hill. It commands a splendid view for many kilometers round about. Large quantities of sherds were found, dating to the 23rd-20th century B. C. In addition, there were large numbers of Iron Age sherds dating to the 13th-6th century B. C. Two ancient cisterns are visible on the top of the hill on the north side. There must be others under the debris. We were unable to ascertain whether or not there is a spring in the vicinity.

On this site, as elsewhere in the regions of Transjordan which we have thus far explored, the gap of approximately 600 years between the early Bronze Age and the Iron Age occupations has prevented the formation of a real *tell* by the process we have already described. One of the striking differences between ancient sites in Palestine and Transjordan, we may recall, is just this frequency of *tulul* in Palestine and their absence in most of Transjordan. An exception is made for the Jordan River Valley. The conclusion which this phenomenon seems to compel is that when at the beginning of the Iron Age the Edomites, Moabites, Ammonites, and Amorites emerged upon the scene in Transjordan as sedentary peoples, they found no ancient sites which had not long previously been destroyed and razed to the ground. When they did build upon the ruins of their early Bronze Age predecessors, as for instance at Arair or Baluah, they either sank the foundations of their buildings down to the original ground-level through whatever ruins may have remained, as at Arair, or they practically swept the ground clean of such remains and then built from the original group-level up, as at Baluah. In all the areas we have thus far explored in Transjordan from South Gilead southward, not a single *tell* or other site had been found containing an uninterrupted sequence of pottery from before 2200 B. C. to and through about 600 B. C.

One of the most interesting early Bronze Age sites in Transjordan was found by Jerash, the site of Gerasa, the great Roman city of the Decapolis. Unusual importance was attached to it because of the fact that it had so long been sought for. Situated in the midst of fertile farm lands in which strong and steady springs flow, and close to an extensive forest region where one can still ride for hours in leafy shade, Jerash would seem to have been occupied from earliest historical times on. Nevertheless, and despite numerous seasons of excavation at Gerasa proper by the joint expeditions of the British School of Archaeology at Jerusalem and later the American Schools of Oriental Research with Yale University, for a long time no traces of settlement were found there which could possibly be dated to the pre-Hellenistic period. "Indeed," as Kraeling, the editor of the final report on the excavations there under the title of *Gerasa, City of the Decapolis,* points out, " the earliest piece of strictly contemporary evidence for the city's history is still an inscribed lead weight of the year 10/11 A. D." [1] He assumes, however, " that the site was occupied at an early date, but how early and by what settlers we can only conjecture, for information bearing upon this point has not yet been discovered," and also that the earliest settlement, wherever it was located, " was in all probability no more than a small village of shepherds and tillers of the soil." [2] Discoveries made in the Jerash region shortly after the publication of this valuable report give basis in fact to this assumption, at the same time showing why the earliest settlement was not found within the limits of Gerasa proper, and indeed why it could not be found there.

On the afternoon of June 21, 1939, we crossed to the east side of Jerash and clambered on top of the outer wall of Roman Gerasa in order to point out to Dr. Walter Lowdermilk, Chief of Research of the Soil Conservation Bureau of the United States Department of Agriculture, how the soil which had been washed down from the slopes east of the wall was now in many instances flush with the top of the wall, and in some places had flowed over the wall and mounted to the top of its inner face. This amount of soil erosion had taken place in spite of the ancient terraces which still protect the hillsides around Jerash, but which have been almost completely neglected, probably since the end of the Byzantine period. Without these terraces, many of which, as we were to see, were built in pre-Hellenistic times, the hillsides around Jerash would long ago have been completely eroded, and would present the barren aspect common to so many slopes in Transjordan, robbed of their good top-soil and in many cases also of their sub-soil through the abuse and neglect of the inhabitants during the course of many centuries.

On top of the Roman wall we saw some Roman sherds, including pieces of sigillata which had been washed down from house sites undoubtedly once situated on the slopes above it. Among these sherds, however, we suddenly noticed, while walking along the top of the wall at its northeast corner, a single fragment of pottery which could be dated indubitably to $\pm$ 2000 B. C. One sherd does not make a settlement, but it does lead one to suppose that such a settlement existed nearby. Looking about now very carefully, we saw a hill less than 200 meters away from the northeast corner of the Roman wall of Gerasa. It looked indeed as if it might be the location of an ancient

[1] Kraeling, *Gerasa,* p. 27.
[2] *Ibid.,* pp. 27, 28.

site, if it were not merely a natural, isolated ridge which, obviously, it had always previously been considered to be.

A careful examination of the slopes leading up to the top of the hill was undertaken, and it very soon became apparent that the single sherd found on the top of the Roman wall was not a lonely waif which had strayed far from home. It was one of many whose history extended from the 23rd to the 20th century B. C. As we ascended the slopes to the top of the hill, it was seen that they were anciently terraced, and so strongly that the terraces have sufficed to hold the earth in place to this very day. As a result, the slopes of the hill are still cultivated from the bottom to the top, as they were about 4000 years ago. It is quite possible that some of the terraces on the slopes of this hill were reenforced or built anew during Roman and Byzantine times. Some Roman and Byzantine sherds were found. Most of the terraces, however, appear to belong to the first stage of agricultural settlement on this hill which has left a record behind it, namely to the early Bronze Age, when also the rich little valley immediately north of Jerash must have been cultivated.

The walled-in area on top of the hill is about 180 meters long, and measures about 78 meters at its widest point near its north end, narrowing down to about 50 meters near its south end. There is a strong spring at the foot of the hill, which the builders of Roman Gerasa walled in beautifully, and which is still used today by the population of the Circassian-Arab village of Jerash. The reason, therefore, why the early settlement had not previously been found within the confines of Roman Gerasa, and why it could not be found there, was that its members chose the more easily defensible, and at the same time the more healthy location on the hill, overlooking the spring, rather than the water-soaked, malaria-ridden location at its foot (Fig. 65).

A sufficient number of early Bronze Age sites has now been discovered to enable one to say that a considerable proportion of them follow a certain pattern of construction. Wherever there is a strong spring or other source of water, and a high, completely isolated, flat-topped hill with good soil, located preferably but not necessarily in the midst of the fertile region, there one may expect to find a walled site belonging to the 23rd-20th centuries B. C. The inhabitants of Transjordan during this period were predominantly an agricultural people. They used much excellent, if on the whole coarse, handmade pottery, and lived under a political system of apparently disunited feudal city-states. In their day the land was obviously flowing with milk and honey, rich in grain, and replete with wine. The limits of cultivation were extended even to difficult *wadi*-slopes.

It was a land which evidently excited the envy of outsiders. About 1900 B. C. this entire civilization extending south of the Jerash region and

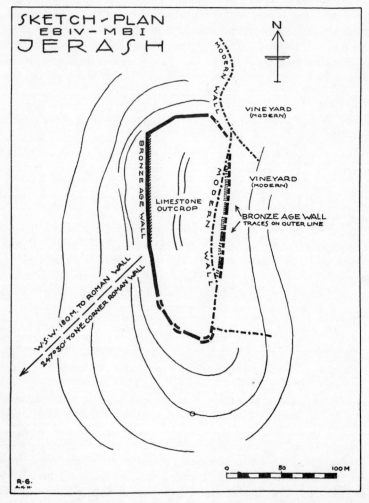

Fig. 65. Sketch plan of early Bronze Age Jerash.

south of the Wadi Zerqa was utterly destroyed, possibly by the Hyksos. Some few places continued to exist till about 1750 B. C. One may surmise also that there was a good deal of rivalry between the numerous settlements of this period, and that their protective walls were at least as much directed against their neighbors as against foreign invaders. Certainly they do not seem to have been sufficiently confederated to withstand the onslaught of the organized army which moved against them, and which was able in one swift march through the land to lay waste all of them.

II

At the beginning of the 13th century B. C. a new agricultural civilization appeared, as we have already noted, belonging to the Edomites, Moabites, Ammonites, and Amorites. Although lost in the haze of ancient history, these peoples were fully as real as the Israelites and the Judaeans. The latter had gifted writers who chronicled, sometimes in much detail and other times merely in outline, the history of their people as illustrative material for the theological purposes of the Bible. Fate has kept both people and Book alive. The historians among their contemporaries on the other side of the Jordan were probably equally gifted, and must also have kept historical records similar to the " Book of the Wars of the Lord " and other source-books referred to in the Bible. They may or may not have had theologians similar to those of Israel and Judah who culled materials from these archives, in order to compile in fixed form for general edification their religious beliefs and practices and principles. Unfortunately, these documents, or others of different literary nature, which must have existed among these ancient kingdoms in Transjordan, have not been handed down into our time by living tradition, any more than the " Book of Yashar " has been preserved. But the fact that we do not possess them can hardly be interpreted to mean that they did not exist.

Even if extensive excavations were undertaken at many sites in Edom or Moab or Ammon or Gilead, there is little hope that writings on parchment or leather or other perishable materials will have escaped the ravages of time. Inscriptions on stone or pottery can, however, withstand moisture and chemical action, and indeed have already been found at various places in Transjordan. Sometimes even writing in ink on such materials may through accident escape destruction. As a matter of fact, in Transjordan more important literary material has already been found accidentally on the surface than has been discovered in excavations. One thinks of the famous Moabite stele found at Dhiban, just north of the Wadi Mojib, which is the longest single literary document outside the Bible dealing with the early history of Palestine and Transjordan in the Iron Age. On it, incised in beautifully cut, ancient Moabite (Hebrew) characters, is the account of how

Mesha, king of Moab, regained the independence of his country from Ahab, king of Israel. One thinks also of the famous stele found at Baluah near the Wadi Mojib, assigned to the 12th century B. C., whose worn lines of inscription can unforunately no longer be read (Fig. 66).

Fig. 66. Egyptianized stele from Baluah in Moab.

Let it not be thought, therefore, that so far as any of the trappings of culture are concerned, the Edomites or Moabites, or any of their contemporaries in Transjordan, were backward, or that they possessed a civilization less developed than that which flourished on the west side of the Jordan. In most respects, all these groups developed similar cultures, spoke and wrote essentially the same western Semitic language, worshipped the same fertility gods, and were of the same or closely related ethnic stock.

Why it was that an inspired handful of religious geniuses in Israel and Judah developed the idea of one great and good god, and that the people of the Book has in a way maintained itself to this very day, while the contemporary kingdoms and peoples of the Other Side of the Jordan have long since disappeared into the limbo of the past, is explained by the religious as the result of the handiwork of God. By the skeptical, it is considered the result of an irrational accident of history, a sort of *glücklicher Zufall*, which might possibly be understood as an ordered event were we in possession of all the inter-related facts of history. To both groups the finds of archaeological research must be very welcome.

The Semites who took possession of Transjordan at the very end of the 14th or the beginning of the 13th century B. C., probably partly absorbed and partly drove out the Bedouins who since about 1900 B. C. had been the masters of the land. For some reason or other, the latter had not been able or had not been willing to affect the change in their status of civilization which the ownership of the soil would have enabled them to do. With the kingdoms of Egypt and Assyria weakened, and no longer in a position to exercise control over greater Palestine, both sides of the Jordan, whether occupied or not by peoples in the agricultural stage of civilization, were open for invasion and settlement by Bedouins or semi-nomadic peoples. They are perpetually land hungry, and the desert areas in which they are wont to wander never suffice for their numbers and their needs.

The new occupants of the land soon broke up into natural groups. This was conditioned partly perhaps by the fact that they represented originally separate tribes, however closely related in general they may have been to each other. Today, for instance, we find the Beni Sakar tribe in control of large areas in northern Transjordan, and the Howeitat tribe in control of much of southern Transjordan. Fully as important, however, for the partition of Transjordan into the kingdoms of Edom, Moab, Ammon, and the two Amorite kingdoms of Gilead, were the natural land divisions of the country. It is bounded on the west by the Wadi Arabah, the Dead Sea, and the Jordan River Valley, jeweled at the top by the lakes of Galilee and Huleh. On the east and south, it is bounded by the desert. These kingdoms were marked off in the main from each other by the wide and deep natural boundaries of the Wadi Hesa (the River Zered), the Wadi Mojib (the River Arnon), the Wadi Zerqa (the River Jabboq), and the Wadi Yarmuk, counting from south to north.

Within these limits, the kingdoms of the Other Side of the Jordan

developed swiftly during the Iron Age. The main period of their development, as indicated also by the excavations of Crowfoot at Baluah, extended
between the 13th and the 8th century B. C., after which a period of deteriora-
tion set in, culminating in complete destruction in the 6th century B. C.
These were highly advanced, strongly organized, internally well integrated
kingdoms. The land was dotted with well built stone villages and towns.
The borders of their kingdoms, which can now be accurately fixed, were
fortified by strong fortresses, built usually on eminences and commanding
a view of each other. Their agriculture was intensive, their pottery well-
made, their commerce sensibly ordered, their literature in all probability of
no mean order, if one may draw inferences from the inscription of Mesha
or the background of the Book of Job. The wealth of these kingdoms,
even under Assyrian domination, may be judged from the tribute paid to
Esarhaddon. Edom paid 12 manas of silver in comparison with 10 manas
of silver paid by Judah; Ammon paid 2 manas of gold; Moab payed 1
mana of gold. The greatness of these kingdoms was, in a word, very real,
however scant the literary remains and memory of their existence have
chanced to be. The civilization of the ancient Near East can certainly not
be comprehended without drawing their history into the orbit of careful
attention.

III

The archaeological survey of Edom soon revealed why it was that not
without permission might a foreign group enter its territory. The permission refused, the applicants for entry must perforce turn aside as the
Israelites were compelled to do. Strong fortresses barred the way on all the
frontiers of Edom, and of Moab north of it. The high, comparatively
fertile and well watered Edomite plateau ends suddenly in the south, with
sheer or precipitous walls and slopes marking the fall to the desert of the
Wadi Hismeh, which stretches to the Red Sea and Arabia (Fig. 67). We had
thought that some Edomite outposts might have existed in this desert to
protect the caravan routes which must have led through it and the Wadi
Yitm to the Wadi Arabah and the Red Sea, or via the Wadi Ramm into
interior Arabia. However, at no place in the desert were any Edomite
remains to be located.

There were, to be sure, numerous paths and tracks through *wudyan*
leading down into the Wadi Arabah directly westward from the Edomite
plateau, which caravans could follow down to the Red Sea. The apparent
absence, however, of Edomite outposts along the caravan tracks leading
through that part of the Wadi Hismeh desert below and south of the

Edomite plateau, which might be accounted as belonging to the Edomite "sphere of interest," probably means that the Edomite caravans were accompanied by armed escorts whenever necessary, even as pilgrim caravans are today. Furthermore, the desert south of the Edomite plateau was in itself a great barrier to the advance of large armies or large groups of people, such as the Israelites, on the move into the richer and fertile parts of Edom proper. The main line of defenses, however, on this front was formed by a series of strong forts.

Fig. 67. Overlooking Wadi Hismeh from Neqb Shtar at the south end of the Edomite plateau.

Near the western edge of the southern limit of the Edomite plateau, on top of an elevation overlooking the Wadi Hismeh, we found the ruins of a strong Edomite fortress, called Khirbet Neqb Shtar or Khirbet Ras en-Neqb. It dominates the main caravan track leading from the Wadi Hismeh to the Jebel Shera, as the southwest part of the Edomite plateau is known. Khirbet Neqb Shtar is more or less in the form of a decagonal oval, with the entrance on the east side between two large rectangular towers. The fortress measures approximately 130 by 117 meters. There appear originally to have been towers and buttresses strengthening the angles of the walls. The site is, however, in such an advanced state of ruin, that little more can be done now than to sketch the course of the outside walls of the fortress. The inside area is filled with a hopeless jumble of ruins, some of which have been turned into sheep folds and goat pens. A number of Iron Age sherds of Edomite type were found, similar to many picked up at the Iron Age sites in the Wadi Arabah. Near the west side of the fortress was a tumbled-in cistern. The hillsides immediately below Khirbet Neqb Shtar seem originally to have been terraced. We were told that there were two springs in the neighborhood, Ain Ibn Suri and Ain Jemam.

About 3 kilometers to the northeast of Khirbet Neqb Shtar, situated on top of a hill commanding a fine view over the Wadi Hismeh and looking down on Khirbet Neqb Shtar to the southwest, is another Edomite border fortress, called Khirbet Shedeiyid. In the vicinity are several springs. Fields cleared of stones, and traces of numerous ancient terraces, are visible between the two Edomite fortresses, testifying to former cultivation. Khirbet Shedeiyid is surrounded by walls made of large, rudely shaped flint blocks, and measures approximately 160 by 76 meters. It has the form of an irregular rectangle. There are traces of revetments and buttresses supporting the bends in the north and south walls. At the northeast corner and against the east wall are the remains of two rectangular towers, the latter supported by a strong glaçis, or defensive slope. The north face of this tower, where the glaçis has fallen away, reveals the fact that it was built on the header-stretcher system, characteristic of the corners of the great Iron Age Moabite fortress at Baluah. Inside the walls there is a maze of ruined foundations. Numerous Edomite sherds were found belonging to the Iron Age, and there were also some Nabataean and mediaeval Arabic sherds.

The eastern border of the Edomite kingdom was even more strongly protected than the southern, its defenses being marked by a long line of fortresses situated on the highest hills in the arid, uncultivated region between the Desert and the Sown. From one end of the country to the other, it would have been possible to transmit fire or smoke signals in a very short time. Indeed, so well were these fortresses situated, that the members of the modern Cadastral Survey being conducted today by the Transjordanian Government have built cairns on them to serve as major triangulation points. In Nabataean, Roman, and Byzantine times, the line of settlements, fortresses, and police-posts extended much farther east than during the Iron Age, as shown, for example, by the Nabataean Bayir (Wells), the Roman Dajaniyeh, and the essentially Byzantine Umm Rasas (Fig. 68), where some Nabataean and Roman sherds and large numbers of Byzantine sherds were found (Fig. 69). This was possible and inevitable during these later periods, because the number of inhabitants in Transjordan during Nabataean-Roman-Byzantine times far exceeded the figure of

Fig. 68. Umm Rasas.

(Courtesy Air Officer Commanding, Royal Air Force, Middle East).

approximately 300,000 for the Iron Age, and because of superior knowledge of methods of conserving water.

Khirbet Tawil Ifjeij, near the southern end of the eastern frontier, is situated on top of the highest hill in the vicinity, commanding a view for kilometers round about. It is marked by a survey cairn. The fortress itself is a ruined square tower, made of rudely cut basalt blocks. There are

10

three cave cisterns on the west side of the tower, which in their present form probably go back to the Nabataean period. They may originally have been used in the Iron Age period of occupation. Large quantities of Edomite Iron Age sherds were found, in addition to some Nabataean and a few mediaeval Arabic sherds.

About 8 kilometers north-northeast of Khirbet Tawil Ifjeij is another such border fortress, called Rujm Jeheirah. It is on a direct line between a similar fortress called Rujm Hala el-Qareneh to the north-northeast and Khirbet Tawil Ifjeij, both places being visible from it. There were several filled-in cisterns on the site. The garrison stationed at Rujm Jeheirah obtained water both from its cisterns and from the *wudyan* below it, where, as we were informed by Bedouins familiar with the district, water can be found even during the dry season by digging shallow pits down to the sub-surface level. Skins or jars of water may have been brought to some of the garrisons. The much ruined fortress-tower of Rujm Jeheirah measures approximately 13 meters square. The walls are built of roughly hewn flint and basalt blocks, and seem to be about 2.20 meters thick. Against them was built a rough flint block glaçis, parts of which are still in place. Immediately below the base of the ruin, on all its sides except the east, are remnants of walls of small compounds and foundations of a few small stone huts, in which perhaps the families of the members of the garrison may have been housed. In the vicinity of some of the modern border fortresses in Transjordan today one can see the tents or the rude houses in which the families of the guardsmen live. Numerous Iron Age and some Nabataean sherds were found.

Nabataean sherds were to be found throughout the entire length and breadth of the Edomite and Moabite kingdoms on Iron Age sites, as well as on purely Nabataean sites. The Nabataeans, as it were, moved in after the retreating Edomites and Moabites, hoisted their own banner, made more or less extensive repairs, and introduced their own pottery. That is perhaps not quite accurately put, in the sense that it is not to be imagined that all of the Edomites emigrated *en bloc* out of their former territory to settle in southern Palestine, where the district in which they lived became known as Idumaea. Actually the picture of what happened is considerably different. Many of the Edomites were undoubtedly pushed out by the infiltrating Nabataeans, and others had probably been driven out, even before the accession of the Nabataeans to power, by the Assyrians, Babylonians, and Persians. It is, however, no more reasonable to assume that all the Edomites left or were expelled from Edom, or all the Moabites from Moab, than it is correct to say that all the Judaeans left or were expelled from their homes as a result of similar conquests.

There must have been many pure-blooded descendants of the Edomites of the once strong Edomite kingdom, who intermarried with the Nabataeans and eventually to all intents and purposes were effectively absorbed by them. There was after all a close blood relationship between the Edomites and Nabataeans, as indeed there was between Judaeans and Edomites and later on Idumaeans. The nature of the mutual relationship of these groups, and an interesting cycle of history, can be no better illustrated than by calling to mind the marriage of Herod Antipas, the son of Herod the Great, of Idumaean origin, to the daughter of the Nabataean king, Aretas IV,— and her flight from him. It is quite likely, therefore, that many of the former Edomite fortresses and police-posts were occupied by garrisons composed either in part or even completely of Nabataeanized Edomites, just as in a partly contemporary period the throne of Judaea was occupied by Judaized Idumaeans. Similarly it may be said that many former Moabite sites were not only occupied by Nabataeans, but were repossessed by Nabataeanized Moabites.

The northern and western boundaries of the kingdom of Edom were no less strongly protected than the eastern and southern, although there were not actually as many fortresses and police-posts. In the first place, the danger of Bedouin invasion was not so great from the west, and was non-existent from the north, and in the second place the deep canyon of the Wadi Hesa and the inhospitable rift of the Wadi Arabah were in themselves formidable barriers to would-be invaders. Nevertheless strong posts protected these fronts also. The possibility that Edomite power once extended into parts of southern Palestine is suggested by a number of Biblical verses which definitely locate Edom-Seir on the west side of the Arabah. All these verses, however, in their present form must be dated to the exilic period or later. They reflect the Idumaean settlement in southern Palestine which the author of Deuteronomy 23, 8 probably had in mind when he said: *You shall not abominate* (i. e. consider as outside the pale of the community) *an Edomite, because he is your brother,* meaning those Idumaeans who had been Judaized and had become Yahweh worshippers.

IV

The boundaries of Moab were fully as strongly fortified as those of Edom, affording further evidence as to why the Israelites were compelled to pass around these two kingdoms when permission was refused them to travel through. The western boundary of Moab was formed by the Dead Sea, the southern by the Wadi Hesa, the eastern by the desert. Some of the eastern outposts appeared even more formidable than the related Edomite ones, because they were better preservd.

One of them is Qasr el-Al. Its position made it one of the most important fortresses of the border defense system on the east front. It also controlled the descent to the Wadi Mojib, which at the time of the advent of the Israelites formed the north boundary of the kingdom of Moab. The *qasr* measures 20 by 16.50 meters, and its west wall is still 18 courses high in places, amounting to 6.80 meters, with the other walls almost as high. The corners of the walls are laid in the header-stretcher system. Very large building blocks were used. There are about half a dozen cisterns on the east side of the fortress. It is a maze of fallen walls of rooms, which have been further disturbed by the burial activities of the Bedouins who inter their dead there. Among the ruins we found numerous Iron Age, many Nabataean, and some Byzantine sherds. All the fortresses for many kilometers round about are visible from Qasr el-Al. On the neighboring hills are the ruins of small watch-towers, which were probably integrated into the border defense system of which Qasr el-Al was evidently a keypost (Fig. 70).

About 5 kilometers south-southwest of Qasr el-Al, and visible from it, is Qasr Abu el-Kharaq. It is another strongly built and well preserved frontier fortress situated on a rise, and commanding an excellent view of the countryside round about it (Fig. 71). There is no habitation in the vicinity of these fortresses today. There was probably never any cultivation of the inhospitable slopes on top of which most of them are located. Their existence was justified by the police and military purposes they served. Qasr Abu el-Kharaq measures 22 by 18 meters. Near the east end of the north wall of the *qasr* is a large, intact doorway, with remnants of what may have been a platform in front of it, and steps leading up to it. The west end of this north wall is preserved to a height of 22 courses, well over 8 meters. The corners of the building are constructed in the header and stretcher system, from two to three headers being required as at Qasr el-Al to equal the length of a stretcher. Towards the south end of the west wall is a small opening near the bottom of the wall, leading into an underground passage. Fallen debris prevented a further examination of its course. The west wall is still 23 courses high. A large number of Iron Age sherds and a smaller number of Nabataean sherds were found.

The Nabataeans and the Romans after them not only took over the Iron Age fortresses they found when they gained possession of the land, but frequently added new ones of their own. Thus about 4 kilometers east-southeast of Qasr Abu Kharaq is the very large fortress-caravanserai of

Fig. 70. Qasr el-Al, Iron Age fortress at the
northeast corner of Moab.

Fig. 71. Qasr Abu el-Kharaq, Moabite border fortress.

Qasr Besheir, 56.75 by 54.45 meters, which is Roman in origin (Fig. 72). It has four corner towers, each three stories high, and a tower on each side of the entrance in the center of the southwest wall. There is a series of rooms, originally two stories high, along the inside face of each wall. On the southwest side of the *qasr* are several cisterns, and to the west of it a large reservoir constructed of well cut stones. Over the doorway is a Latin inscription, according to which the *qasr* is described as a *castra praetorii Mobeni,* that is, as the camp of the praetorium of Moab. According to this inscription, the *qasr* was built under Diocletian and replaced a sort of rest house in which government officers could find quarters while on official

Fig. 72.   Qasr Besheir.

journeys.   Practically no sherds were found.   The Roman site of Qasr Besheir is to be brought into relationship with the great Roman camp known today as el-Lejjun, about 18 kilometers to the southwest (Fig. 73).   On the hill above el-Lejjun and its splendid spring was found, it may be recalled, a very large early Bronze Age site, with a series of standing monoliths by it.

We have already pointed out that the north boundary of the kingdom of Moab at the time of the advent of the Israelites was marked by the Wadi Mojib. This was not always so. Numbers 21, 26-30 inform us that after the " first " king of Moab had been defeated by Sihon, king of the Amorites (in the south half of Gilead), the Amorite king made Heshbon his place of residence.   He had conquered or perhaps reconquered that part of

Moabite territory which extended from Heshbon as far south as the Arnon (Wadi Mojib). This line stretching eastward from beyond the north end of the Dead Sea was subsequently to mark the limit of the northern extent

Fig. 73. Lejjun.

(Courtesy Air Officer Commanding, Royal Air Force, Middle East).

of the Nabataean kingdom in southern Transjordan. Both sides of the Arnon were strongly fortified in the Iron Age, but while the Israelites must have considered the Edomite and Moabite border fortifications too formidable to cope with, they attempted and succeeded in entering and conquering the kingdom of Sihon. At the time of their arrival, it extended from the

Arnon to the Jabboq, and from the wilderness to the Jordan, according to Judges 11, 22.

It was not till the end of the reign of Ahab of Israel that Mesha of Moab was able to regain the independence of his kingdom from the Israelite king, and restore the ancient boundaries of Moab to the limits which had prevailed before Sihon had detached the section north of the Arnon. Madeba, Nebo, Jahaz, sites mentioned among others in the Moabite stone, reflect the northern extent of Mesha's recovered territory which corresponded with that of his remote predecessor, the " first " king of Moab. The restoration of greater Moab marked the height of its development. Its later history was characterized by a rapid decline, which culminated in the end of Moab as an independent kingdom in the 6th century B. C.

V

The description above of the extent of the kingdom of Sihon in South Gilead is in general but not completely accurate, particularly with regard to the west and east boundaries, described in Judges 11, 22 as extending " from the wilderness to the Jordan." Actually, as we learn from Joshua 12, 3, Sihon controlled a large corridor consisting of the entire east side of the Jordan, extending from the east side of the north half of the Dead Sea to the east side of the south end of the Lake of Galilee. Furthermore, the east boundary of the kingdom of Sihon does not quite correspond with " the wilderness." A closer definition is given in Joshua 12, 2 where it is stated that the Israelites conquered

Sihon, king of the Amorites, who dwelt in Heshbon, ruling from Aroer which is on the edge of the plateau overlooking the Nahal Arnon,—with its boundary line commencing in the midst of the actual nahal bed—, over the (south) half of Gilead as far as the Nahal Jabboq, the boundary of the Beni Ammon.

According to this verse the east boundary of the kingdom of Sihon and thus the west boundary of the kingdom of Ammon is to be identified with the Jabboq, that is the Wadi Zerqa. However, in Judges 11, 22 the northern boundary of Sihon's kingdom is also identified with the Jabboq. The explanation is simple. The Jabboq formed both the eastern and northern boundaries of the kingdom of Sihon, in the first instance being that part of the present Wadi Zerqa which extends approximately from the south to the north, and in the second instance that part which extends from the east to the west, where it joins the Jordan.

Along all these boundaries strong Iron Age fortifications have been found. The *original* Ammonite kingdom consisted then of the small, fairly fertile strip on the east side of the south-north stretch of the Wadi Zerqa, and extended eastward to the desert. In this narrow strip there were located such Iron Age Ammonite sites as Khirbet Nimrah, Khirbet Sukhneh, Khirbet Breitawi, er-Reseifawi, Khirbet Jeish, esh-Shih, el-Jidi, el-Musaffar, and above all Amman, the Biblical Rabbath Ammon. South of Amman were also several important sites which may have belonged to the Ammonite kingdom, such as es-Sweiwina and Rujm Wasiyeh. That the south-north stretch of the Wadi Zerqa formed the boundary line between the kingdoms of Sihon and Ammon is stated also in Numbers 21, 24:

And Israel smote him (Sihon) by the edge of the sword and took possession of his land from the Arnon to (both stretches of) the Jabboq,—as far (east) as the Beni Ammon, because strong was the boundary of the Beni Ammon.

The fact that the advancing Israelite forces stopped at the east boundary of the kingdom of Sihon, which bordered on the territory of the Ammonites, is reflected also in Deuteronomy 2, 19 and 37, in which last verse we read:

However, to the land of the Beni Ammon you shall not come near, all the slope of the Nahal Jabboq and the hill cities. . . .

The *hill cities* must refer to the sites in the kingdom of Ammon we have mentioned above, situated in the broken upland district on the east side of the south-north stretch of the Wadi Zerqa.

The north and south limits of the early Ammonite kingdom can be determined generally by the north and south extent of the sites mentioned. The possibility must be considered also that at one time the southern limit of the Ammonite kingdom may have been marked by the eastern stretch of the Arnon. The territory of Og stretched in the main from the east-west stretch of the Jabboq to the Yarmuk, and from the east side of Sihon's corridor along the Jordan to the desert. We have not yet been able to examine this territory archaeologically. The question whether or not these Biblical boundary descriptions may represent idealizations of the territories occupied by Reuben, Gad, and half of the tribe of Manasseh, requires serious consideration.

VI

The interiors of Edom and Moab did not rely for protection solely on the fortresses which guarded their borders. Practically every site throughout the length and breadth of the land either consisted of a great fortress or a strong blockhouse. Sometimes it was marked by a strong central structure around which the houses and tents of the residents were clustered,

all contained within a great enclosing fortification wall.   One such place
is represented by the ruins of Khirbet Remeil in Moab, overlooking the
Wadi Remeil (Fig. 74).   It is one of the best preserved examples of an Iron

Fig. 74.   er-Remeil.

(Courtesy Air Officer Commanding, Royal Air Force, Middle East).

Age fortress placed in a strongly walled compound that we have thus far
discovered in all of our explorations on the Other Side of the Jordan.   The
enclosed area measures about 115 by 70 meters.

At the northeast angle of the outer wall, which is strengthened by a dry
moat around it, are the remains of an elaborate gateway.   The approach to

it seems to have been masked, compelling entrance from the north and south sides. Once inside the fortress-compound, one finds oneself in a confusing maze of ruined house foundations, which, however, assume a semblance of reasonable order when viewed from the air. Particularly noticeable is the large empty space inside the compound, immediately in front of the north side of the blockhouse. One can imagine that it was in this open square that the community gathered for public events, and the judges sat in their seats and listened to the complaints of the villagers and the pleas of the travellers, who used the well-worn track that connected Khirbet Remeil with the Iron Age sites in the neighborhood. Inside and outside the enclosure are the remains of numerous cisterns and cave cisterns.

The dominant feature of Khirbet Remeil is the central blockhouse or fortress. This building measures 18.90 by 15 meters. Its walls are 1.50 meters thick. Although much ruined, the building is still 6 meters high. The corners of the structure are laid in the typical Iron Age header and stretcher system, large blocks being used for the purpose. Despite the constant grubbing that goes on inside its ruins for burial purposes by the Bedouins, this central building is still sufficiently intact, we believe, to furnish a rather complete plan of its rooms, if they could be cleared of the fallen stones which at present obliterate their precise outlines. There is also clear evidence that originally a glaçis was built against the walls of the fortress, lending further strength to this strongly built structure.

Large quantities of Iron Age sherds of all kinds were found inside and outside of the ruins of Khirbet Remeil, including numerous painted sherds of particularly fine quality. It is probable that not all of the inhabitants of the place lived at any one time within its walls. Many of them, as is frequently the practice in Arab villages today, probably lived in tents for long periods of the year away from home, following the crops. Khirbet Remeil is located in what is now an almost completely abandoned region, visited by occasional shepherds with their flocks during the winter and spring, but formerly a fairly thriving agricultural district, in which apparently a good deal of dry farming was carried on.

About 4 kilometers to the northeast of Khirbet Remeil is another great Moabite site called el-Medeiyineh, situated on a knoll, and surrounded by a strong wall, the outlines of which are seen in the air view (Fig. 75). It overlooks the Wadi Themed which is the eastward continuation of the Wadi Remeil. Water is still obtainable by digging shallow pits in the dry bed of the *wadi*. The long, rectangular site, measuring 160 by 40 meters, is further protected by a dry moat, which completely surrounds it. From the air, el-Medeiyineh looks very much like Maiden Castle in England. It is one of the few sites in Transjordan which has the appearance of a *tell,* and where, if stratigraphic excavations were attempted, several successive layers of occupation might be revealed (Fig. 76). Quantities of coarse and

Fig. 75. el-Medeiyineh in the Wadi Themed.

(Courtesy Air Officer Commanding, Royal Air Force, Middle East).

fine, plain and painted Moabite pottery belonging to the Iron Age were found there, in addition to some Nabataean sherds, and some Iron Age figurines.

A site of much interest is that of Khirbet Ayun Musa, several kilometers northeast of Mt. Nebo, known today as Jebel Siyaghah. On top of the mountain are the remains of a Byzantine church which the Franciscans have cleared with loving care. It occupies a fine vantage point, commanding a view of much of the Jordan River Valley and of the hill country of Palestine. The towers of Jerusalem and of Bethlehem can be made out easily with the naked eye. The slopes of Mt. Nebo and the plain stretching below towards the Dead Sea are cultivated in spots, and the region to the southeast and east is quite productive. The land of Moab and the lands of Edom, Ammon, and Gilead were and still are to a large degree fruitful. There are numerous springs, and the soil in the arable areas is good. From

Fig. 76. el-Medeiyineh in the Wadi Themed.

the vantage point of Mt. Nebo, Moses not only viewed the Promised Land to the west of the Jordan, but stood and died in a blessed country to the east of the Jordan.

A steep trail from Mt. Nebo leads down to the Ayun Musa, the Springs of Moses, whose strongly flowing waters irrigate a number of gardens. On top of the steep hill to the northwest, immediately overlooking the springs, are the remains of Khirbet Ayun Musa. It was once surrounded by a strong outer wall, which seems in places to have been supported by a glacis, and was cut off from the broken plateau land to the north by a dry moat. Whether or not the fortress was in existence at the time of Moses or was destroyed by his people, is impossible to say definitely. The likelihood is that there was a fortress there when his travel-worn people arrived at Mt.

Nebo. On the hillsides below the fortress and within its walled area were found large quantities of Iron Age sherds, and also some Nabataean sherds.

VII

The Edomite, Moabite, Ammonite, and Gileadite pottery of the 13th-6th century B. C. bespeaks a highly developed civilization, more or less common to all the Iron Age kingdoms in Transjordan, and the presence of potters skilled in ceramic craft and possessed of high artistic sense. Many of the sherds found were covered with a beautiful red or brown slip, highly polished, and further decorated with horizontal bands of dark brown paint, and sometimes with bands of white-wash between them. This kind of ornamentation is suggestive of that of the Cypro-Phoenician ointment juglets and miniature amphorae, both of imported and native imitations, found in Palestine in the first part of the Iron Age.

The similarity is not, however, complete. The differences are large enough to compel an individual classification. Indeed, in general one may say that the peculiarities, particularly in ornamentation, of Edomite and Moabite and related pottery in Transjordan, set it in a category of its own, despite its close connections in many ways with contemporary pottery in Western Palestine. This is all the more surprising in view of the fact that there is no distinguishable difference, except the occasional ones of texture and clay, between the early Bronze Age pottery of Eastern and Western Palestine.

The distinctiveness of some of the Iron Age pottery of the Other Side of the Jordan may perhaps be ascribed to influences emanating from Syria via the trade-route that followed the " King's Highway." The orientation of Edom, Moab, Ammon, and Gilead, for economic and geographical reasons, may be said to be chiefly to the north and south rather than to the west, that is mainly to Syria and Arabia rather than to Palestine. It is evident from much of the pottery found at Solomon's seaport and factory town of Ezion-geber, that it can only be understood in its essential uniqueness by recognizing that it must represent a distinctive facet of the intimate cultural connection of Ezion-geber with Arabia and Sinai (Fig. 77).

It may be emphasized with regard to the Iron Age pottery of Edom, Moab, and the other kingdoms of Transjordan, but particularly with regard to the first two because the largest quantities were found there, that its beginnings go back to what would be the end of Late Bronze in Palestine, no later than the first part of the 13th century B. C. Again do archaeological facts bear out the validity of details or of the background of Biblical accounts.   The precedence of the beginnings of Edomite and Moabite pottery, for instance, over those of Israelite pottery, has a direct relationship to the Biblical account in Genesis 31, 31-9, which lists eight Edomite " kings " who reigned in the land of Edom before the Israelites had a king.

It becomes impossible, therefore, in the light of all this new archaeological evidence, particularly when studied in connection with the deposits of historical memory contained in the Bible, to escape the conclusion that the

Fig. 77.   Painted Moabite sherds of the types found at el-Medeiyineh and Khirbet Remeil.

particular Exodus of the Israelites through southern Transjordan could not have taken place before the 13th century B. C.   It will be recalled that the Israelites begged the Edomites and Moabites in vain for permission to travel through these kingdoms on their way to the Promised Land.   The Israelites were compelled to go around them, and finally force their way westward to the Jordan on the north side of the Arnon, which at that time was part of the territory of Sihon, king of the Amorites.   Had the Exodus through southern Transjordan taken place before the 13th century B. C., the Israelites would have found neither Edomite nor Moabite kingdoms, well organized and well fortified, whose rulers could have given or withheld permission to go through their territories. Indeed, the Israelites, had they arrived on the scene first, might have occupied all of Edom and Moab themselves, and left the land on the west side of the Jordan for late comers.

VIII

Of a particularly formidable looking character are many of the Iron Age sites in Ammon and South Gilead, whose history, like that of the contemporary sites in Edom and Moab, extends from the 13th to the 6th century B. C., with the most flourishing period extending down to about the 8th century B. C. An excellent example is Khirbet Morbat Bedran, about 14 kilometers north-northeast of Amman, the present capital of Transjordan, and formerly the capital of the kingdom of Ammon. It is in a once fertile, but now more or less exhausted agricultural region, which is only poorly cultivated in spots. It occupies an area of approximately 280 by 90 meters, and consists of a number of scattered buildings overlooking a small *wadi*. Along the length of the south end of the site, near the top of the *wadi,* are several cisterns. Others are probably buried under the debris.

The individual structures of this ancient village were independently so strong that no outer fortification wall was deemed necessary. Large quantities of Iron Age sherds were found. The walls or foundations of at least twelve massive buildings can still be traced. Today only one family, comprising not more than ten people, lives in a tent on the site, and scratchily cultivates some of the surrounding fields which once were intensively farmed. To give an idea of the size of the buildings at Khirbet Morbat Bedran, we may note the dimensions of one of them. Qasr I measures 15.30 by 17.60 meters, with an annex on the west side which measures 10 by 17.60 meters (Fig. 78). The southwest corner of Qasr I is still 6 courses, 3.40 high.

Of especial interest are the round towers, *rujum malfuf,* at Khirbet Morbat Bedran, which are also to be assigned, with the rest of the site, to the Iron Age,—a conclusion we had previously arrived at from the examination of isolated round towers in the region of Amman. These round towers, merely on the basis of the fact that they looked old and were built in the " megalithic " style, have previously and wrongly been assigned to the Early Bronze Age or earlier. They evidently served, wherever located, as police or lookout towers. It is noteworthy that these round towers have thus far not been found in Western Palestine, and seem indeed to be a peculiarity of the east half of South Gilead.

About 6 kilometers east-southeast of Khirbet Morbat Bedran, situated

11

Fig. 78.   Khirbet Morbat Bedran.

Fig 79.   Khirbet Mudmar, Qasr II.

in the rich valley of the Beq'ah, through which one travels from the south on the way to Jerash, is another " megalithic " site, called Khirbet Mudmar, one of a whole series of places like it in this valley.   It is composed of a number of large, more or less ruined buildings, extending over an area approximately 300 meters in length, and from 60 to 100 meters in width. Among and around the ruins of the buildings were found numerous Iron Age sherds.   There were also several Roman sherds of about the 1st century A. D., as well as some Byzantine and mediaeval Arabic sherds.   The south wall of one of the buildings is still preserved at the corners to a height of 9 courses, or 5.50 meters.   The walls average 2 meters in thickness (Fig. 79).

We have only partly examined the territory of North Gilead stretching between the Wadi Zerqa and the Wadi Yarmuk.   We have already discussed the early Bronze Age site overlooking Jerash.   About $4\frac{1}{2}$ kilometers north-northeast of it, on top of a high, completely isolated hill, we found the ruins of a large Iron Age acropolis, called Khirbet Kibdeh.   Whether or not Khirbet Kibdeh is to be identified with the Iron Age equivalent of Roman Jerash remains an open question.

In this region also we find thus a gap in the history of permanent settlement extending from the end of the 20th to the beginning of the 13th century B. C., and another one from the end of the 6th century until about the 3rd century B. C.   It is significant with regard to the earlier gap in history in Transjordan as far as the Jerash region, that neither the Egyptian lists of towns nor the Tell el-Amarna tablets refer to Eastern Palestine in this period.   Edom and Seir, for instance, are first mentioned in the records of Mernepthah (1225-1215 B. C.) and Ramses III (1198-1167 B. C.).   It may furthermore be mentioned in this connection, that there are no archaeological traces of Horites in either the hill country of Edom or the Wadi Arabah or in southernmost Palestine, unless under Horites are to be understood purely nomadic groups, such as the Edomites must have found and conquered when they entered southern Transjordan.

This break of about 600 years in the history of agricultural civilization is remarkably paralleled in the comparatively modern history of Transjordan by another one lasting about 700 years, from the end of the mediaeval Arabic period to about the beginning of the 20th century A. D.   This is most strikingly true of the history of Jerash itself, which was completely abandoned after the mediaeval Arabic period, and remained unoccupied until little more than 50 years ago.   Then Abdul Hamid settled an energetic Circassian community there, and at other well located, fertile points in the country, such as Amman.   By 1122 A. D. William of Tyre speaks of Jerash as having long been uninhabited.   At this time a garrison of 40 men was temporarily stationed there by the Atabeg of Damascus, and it contrived to transform the temple of Artemis there into a fortress. However, a visitor to the site described the city to the Arabic historian, Yaqut, in the next century as a field of ruins, save for a few water mills, and as completely uninhabited. The history of Amman is much the same as that of Jerash, and the same story could be repeated for all the cities of the Decapolis.

The decay and disappearance, for all practical purposes, of agricultural civilization centering about thriving towns and villages throughout most of Transjordan in our era, can no more be explained by climatic changes than can the phenomena involving the previous periods of abandonment of the sedentary cultivation of the soil. In both instances the explanation must be sought largely in human factors, although our knowledge of the variables conditioning the early gaps is far more meager than that conditioning the recent one. This is not the place to discuss in detail why from the 8th-9th century A. D. to the 19th century A. D., and more particularly from the 12th to the 19th century, Transjordan was marked only by a few settlements, while the Bedouins possessed almost all the land.

Had Transjordan possessed the sacred sites and religious attractions, with the more or less continuous streams of pilgrims and trade interests dependent upon them that Palestine always had, its history would have been far different. It would not then have presented the anomalous picture of a fertile country, rich also in forests and minerals, practically abandoned for a period of many centuries by farmers and tradesmen and journeymen of all kinds. It is really only since the close of the 1914-18 War that under the beneficent rule of the British mandatory government Transjordan is beginning to live up to the promise which her resources and her past history hold for her.

IX

Numerous individual finds have been made during the course of the archaeological survey of Edom and Moab which afford illuminating glimpses into the religious life of the Edomites and Moabites, and which may be taken as characteristic also for the related peoples of Transjordan. Particularly prominent in the pantheon of deities worshipped by them were the gods and goddesses of fertility. The farmers of Edom and Moab and other parts of Transjordan had in their houses crude pottery figurines, representing the gods whose good will they sought. Thus, near Buseirah, which is to be identified with the ancient Edomite town of Bozrah, prominently mentioned in the Bible, there was found a figurine of the fertility goddess

wearing a lamp as a crown, and holding in her hands what seems to be a
sacred loaf of bread. To judge from the saucer-lamp, the figurine may be
assigned to about the 9th-8th century B. C.   The hair is represented by
ridges on the back and sides of the head, with an ornamental row of holes
punched across the forehead immediately below the lamp.   The head of a
similar " lamp " goddess came from the same place (Fig. 80).   Around the
front of the neck is a collar decorated with a double row of punched holes,

Fig. 80.   Figurines from near Buseirah.

while the back and sides of the head are covered with strips of clay representing locks of hair.   The lower left cheek is tattooed with three holes.
The head of a figurine, on which is a saucer lamp of about the 8th century
B. C., very similar to the heads of these Transjordan " lamp-goddesses,"
was found at Ain Shems in Palestine (Fig. 81).

Together with the two " lamp-goddesses " from near Buseirah, there was
found the crude figurine of another stand-goddess, the head of which fitted
separately into the body by means of a prong.   It seems probable that the
arms now broken off were originally crossed in front, with a round or ovoid
object clutched in the hands, as in the case of the first " lamp-goddess "

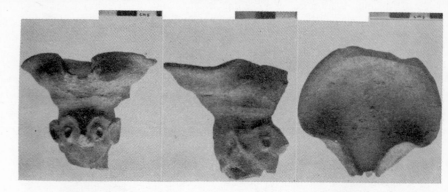

Fig. 81. Head of " lamp-goddess " from Ain Shems.

(Courtesy Elihu Grant and Palestine Archaeological Museum).

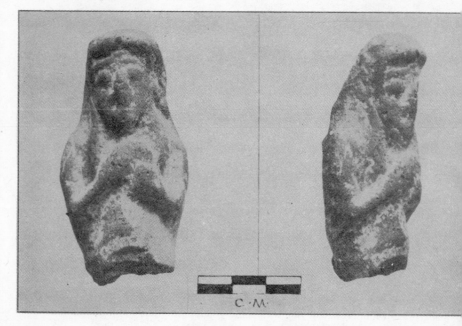

Fig. 82. Figurine from near Mount Nebo.

mentioned above. The heavy ridges above the eyes give a prehistoric look
to the flat-faced, ovoid-shaped head, which is further distinguished by a
protruding proboscis, Sumerian in appearance. This figurine too, may be
assigned to about the 9th-8th century B. C.

Figurines of fertility goddesses holding loaves of bread(?) or some other
sacred object, have been found near Mt. Nebo (Fig. 82) and near Kerak in
Transjordan, and others at Beisan and Megiddo in Palestine (Fig. 83).
Belonging to this latter type of figurine of a fertility goddess are two heads
of figurines found, respectively, at el-Medeiyineh on the Wadi Themed and

(Courtesy of Transjordan
Dept. of Antiquities).

(Courtesy Palestine
Archaeological Museum).

Fig. 83. Female figurines with fertility(?) symbol from near Kerak (left)
and Beisan (right).

Baluah in Transjordan (Fig. 84). The prong by which the latter was
attached to the body is still intact. The large ears, the bulging eyes over
which are long, semicircular, prominent eyebrows, the distended cheeks,
narrow slit of a mouth, long locks of hair, and pointed chin, are like the
features of the more complete pottery figurines of this type.

With these figurines of deities there were sometimes found figurines of
animals, such as the ram's head from Saliyeh, and the bull's head from
el-Medeiyineh (Fig. 85). On the rich dump-heap at el-Medeiyineh there
was found, furthermore, the head of another pottery figurine (Fig. 86),
which represents a Semitic king or diety. The head is skilfully moulded,
every feature being clearly and boldly delineated. The headdress is kept

Fig. 84. Heads of figurines from el-Medeiyineh (left) and Baluah (right).

in place by an *uqal*. Behind and below the ears extend long locks of braided hair. The pointed beard extends from below thick protruding lips. The curved nose, bulging cheeks, with two incisions on the right side, and large slanting eyes complete the picture. Another interesting find made at el-Medeiyineh was part of a pottery figurine of a horse (?), with the legs and arms of a rider still attached to it. A similar fragment found there had only the feet of a rider still attached to it (Figs. 87-88).

Fig. 85. Terracotta heads from Saliyeh (left) and el-Medeiyineh (right).

X

Figurines, inscriptions, steles, pottery fragments, sacred objects, and the ancient sites on which they occur (many of which throughout the length of Transjordan are connected by the " King's Highway "), and also mines and metals,—these are the materials of history gained by gleaning from the surface-ruins still left in Edom, Moab, Ammon, and Gilead. They testify to the reality and to the kind of kingdoms which once existed on the Other Side of the Jordan, alongside of the kingdoms of Israel and Judah. They also tend to make more real such figures as Jepthah of Gilead and his daughter, who was devoted to her father's vow, and Balaam of Ammon, who refused at the behest of Balak, king of Moab, to curse Israel, and Job of Edom, who refused to curse God.

Fig. 86. Head of a Semitic king or deity from el-Medeiyineh.

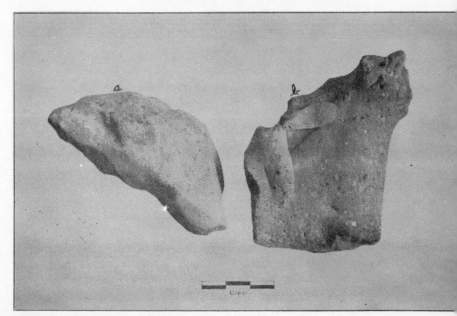

Fig. 87. Fragments of pottery animal figurines, with traces of riders, from el-Medeiyineh.

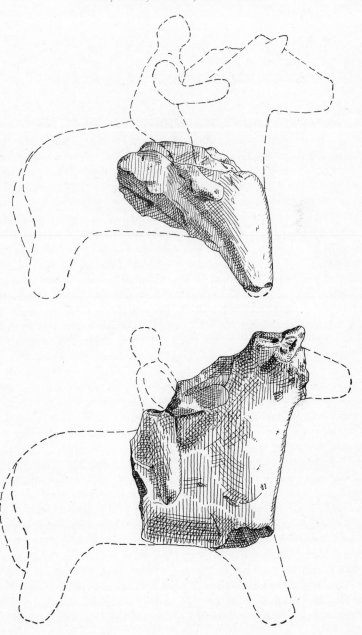

Fig. 88. Reconstructions of the preceding figure.

Chapter VI

THE CIVILIZATION OF THE NABATAEANS

I

Our knowledge of the Nabataean civilization and of the extent and character of the Nabataean kingdom is rapidly increasing. The gifted Nabataeans not only spoke Arabic, but also spoke and wrote an Aramaic dialect, and many of them were also well versed in Greek. They are usually associated with their amazing capital city, Petra. The spectacular rise and development of the Nabataean kingdom to great wealth and power, between the first centuries B. C. and A. D., were due in large part to the fact that it was situated on important trade-routes between Arabia and Syria. Along these routes were carried not only the rich merchandise of southern Arabia, but also valuable products which had been transported to Arabia from Africa, India, and even China. Heavily laden caravans converged on Petra. Merchandise was re-expedited from Petra to Egypt, and to Greece and Italy via Gaza, and to Syria. There must have been also much trade with Persia. Goods were also sent directly to various countries from ports on the eastern arm of the Red Sea, and from emporia in Arabia. The Nabataeans waxed wealthy in part through the heavy taxes imposed on the goods in transit through their territory It is, however, a serious mistake to think of the Nabataeans as merely a group of rich traders and caravaneers, banded together in a loosely organized state, which centered about the tremendous merchandise mart of Petra, for the purpose of keeping the all important trade-routes open and protecting the numerous caravans which traversed them.

The Nabataean kingdom was highly organized and intensively occupied, and was concerned with much more than caravan trade. Not only did the Nabataeans have numerous fixed posts guarding their trade-routes, such as the one at Bayir (Wells), or at Ain Shellaleh in the Wadi Ramm, or along the trade-route leading through the Wadi Arabah, but there were also long lines of frontier posts and watch-towers and sometimes large key fortresses. These guarded the boundaries along the fertile parts of the kingdom, protecting particularly the rich, cultivated, plateau-lands of what had once been the territories of the kingdoms of Moab and Edom against Bedouin invasion. The Nabataeans adopted the methods of defense and organization which the Edomites and Moabites had worked out before them, improving upon them,

158

and enlarging their scope. On practically every one of the numerous towers and frontier posts and fortresses of the long line of defenses marking the eastern boundaries of the Edomite and Moabite kingdoms, stretching from the top of Neqb esh-Shtar to the Wadi Hesa, and from the Wadi Hesa to the northeastern corner of Moab, we found Nabataean sherds in addition to Moabite or Edomite sherds. The earlier buildings were either directly taken over by the Nabataeans, sometimes with the addition of super-

Fig. 89. Nabataean dam at Rekhemtein.

structures of their own, or new constructions were erected directly next to, or enclosing, or in the immediate vicinity of the older ones. In addition, the Nabataeans built many new fortresses and watch-towers of their own on previously unoccupied sites. Their power extended at one time as far north as Damascus, and as far south as Medain Saleh. The vigorous Nabataean kings played an active role in the political life of the countries immediately bordering their kingdom. Herod Antipas was to rue the day when he divorced his Nabataean wife, the daughter of Aretas IV (9 B. C.- 40 A. D.), and Paul of Tarsus was to feel the power of this same Aretas when he came out of the desert.

In art, architecture, and engineering, perhaps in literature, certainly in ceramics, the Nabataeans were one of the most gifted peoples known in history. No other people in Syria, Transjordan, and Arabia pushed the boundaries of agriculture as far into the desert as they did. Nor did any other people so blithely and successfully tackle mountain sides and dry river beds, for the purpose of catching and conserving the heavy rains of a short but extremely wet season. The prospect of carving temples and tombs and dwellings out of the native rock seems to have daunted the Nabataean architects not at all.

In the Wadi Ramm, situated in the great Wadi Hismeh desert, which stretches south of the Edomite plateau into Arabia, we came several years ago upon a small, square, completely ruined Nabataean tower, called Rekhemtein, by the side of which were some Nabataean sherds. Several hundred meters south of this Nabataean tower is a small, gray, sandstone hill, whose curved north side has been smoothed and hardened by the play of the elements, and to a certain extent by the hand of man. A wedge-shaped fissure near the east end of this side of the hill had been dammed up by a wall at its lower end (Fig. 89), creating an excellent reservoir for the rain-water flowing through the fissure, which would otherwise have gone to waste. Channels cut into the sides of the hill on either side of the fissure led additional quantities of rain water into the reservoir. A sufficient supply of water was obtained thus to provide for the needs of the small garrison that policed this Nabataean outpost. The method of conserving water at Rekhemtein is but one small example in many of the industry and skill of the Nabataeans, who could maintain themselves through such means even in the desert (Fig. 90).

Much more striking, naturally, are the rock-hewn structures of Petra including temples, houses, tombs, cisterns, aqueducts and altars. About 5 kilometers north-northwest of Petra is one of its suburbs, called el-Bared. It is a miniature Petra, containing many of the natural and architectural beauties of that site in small compass. In the Ard el-Beida, immediately opposite el-Bared, we came upon an entire complex of Nabataean cisterns and catch-basins hewn out of the rock. One of these large cisterns, at the bottom of a high, perpendicularly faced hill, is Bir Beida (Fig. 91). Rain water falling on the hill was deflected into the cistern at its foot. A small hill near it had been almost completely utilized to provide burial chambers and cisterns (Fig. 92). We visited el-Bared in the spring, and some of the cisterns still contained water from the recent rains. It is easy to see that by multiplying these instances literally by the hundred, huge quantities of water could be stored, serving large numbers of people and numerous herds throughout the dry months of the year.

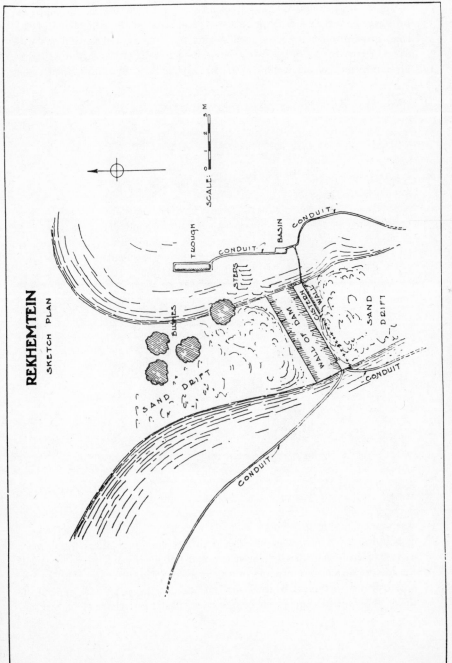

Fig. 90. Rekhemtein sketch plan.

On the west side of the Ard Beida, a narrow ravine cutting through the hills widens out into the Siq (street) of el-Bared. On either side of the cool, grass-covered street is a succession of temples, tombs, and cisterns carved out of the solid, multi-colored sandstone walls of the ravine. Flights of stairs, most of them broken off midway, lead to dwellings, tombs and

Fig. 91. Nabataean cistern, Bir Beida.

reservoirs, hanging so to speak in mid-air. The sophisticated attractiveness of temples and tombs, some of them with free standing pillars which look as if they had been placed in position, and not merely left there when all the intervening masses of stone were cut away (Fig. 93), and others with architraves with typical triglyph and metope designs (Fig. 94), and all of them with horned capitals on columns or pilasters of classical Nabataean pattern, adds to the natural beauty of el-Bared. At the point where the Siq el-Bared near its western end narrows so abruptly that the opposite walls seem almost to touch, a flight of steps leads up through the opening between the walls to the broken plateau beyond, which extends for some distance to

Fig. 92. Khirbet Umm Qeseir, a hill converted by the Nabataeans into a series of burial chambers and cisterns.

the west before the descent into the Wadi Arabah begins. In some of the buildings at el-Bared were beautiful murals (Fig. 95).

Another site distinguished by the genius of the Nabataeans for engineering skill in water conservation, enabling them to live where others could not survive, is called Sela (the Rock), situated only a few kilometers west-northwest of Buseirah (the Biblical Bozrah). Although the name of Sela

12

Fig. 93. Nabataean tomb at el-Bared, looking north.

Fig. 94. Nabataean tomb at el-Bared, looking south.

Fig. 95. Nabataean mural painting from el-Bared.

may well be handed down from early Biblical times, since it is possible to show that this was originally an Edomite before it became a Nabataean site, it is not to be confused with the Biblical Sela, which we have identified with Umm el-Biyarah in Petra. Opposite the small modern village of Sela, with its springs known as the Moyet Dleib, and across the small Wadi

Fig. 96. Nabataean dam below Sela, looking southeast.

el-Hirsh, is visible to the northwest the completely isolated, jagged, precipitous hill of Sela, with the ancient site of the same name on top of it. It was once the center of an intensively cultivated area, which is now almost completely desolate. The hillside sloping down to the Wadi el-Hirsh below the modern village was once completely terraced, but only a few of the terraces are intact and cultivated today. A narrow cleft down this hill-

Fig. 97. Siq of Nabataean Sela near Buseirah (Bozrah).

side, widening at the bottom of the slope, was formerly dammed up by a strong masonry wall thrown across its outlet. At one time thus a considerable amount of water was impounded, in almost exactly the same fashion as at Rekhemtein (Fig. 96).

A staircase up the slope of the hill leads into a narrow *siq*, which seems to be the only entrance to ancient Sela (Fig. 97). Most of Sela on the hill is given over to catchment basins, cisterns, and some houses, hewn for the most part directly out of the solid sandstone. Enough water was caught and kept on top of Sela, easily to supply the needs of a community of at least a hundred people for a year. Dominating the entire site is a small, prominent, cone-shaped projection which, too, was impressed into the service of storing water. In the center a deep cistern had been sunk. No people other than the Nabataeans, in all probability, would have thought of utilizing the cone for this purpose (Fig. 98).

This cone-shaped outcrop drops precipitously on its northwest side. Steps cut into the rock lead down its southeast side to a fairly flat ridge, where we found the remains of a *birkeh*. At the east and southeast ends of this ridge were the ruins of private houses. They were partly hewn out of the solid rock, and partly constructed of rectangular sandstone blocks. The houses were plastered on the inside, and some of them were pretentiously painted with brilliant red, blue, and green patterns.

At the east end of the ridge there was a house, the main east room of which had a vaulted roof, still partly intact. Most of the room was hewn out of the solid rock. A large doorway leads from the west side of this room to an entrance chamber or small courtyard on a lower level. In the middle of it is a very large cistern. The rain water from off the roof of the vaulted room ran into a small rock-hewn reservoir behind it, whence it was led through a rock-cut channel into the cistern, via a settling basin. When the cistern was full, the channel could be blocked off, and the water diverted through an aperture in the south wall to a reservoir (Fig. 99). It was particularly in the vaulted room of this house that remnants of brilliantly painted plaster could be seen. The painting seems to have been done in horizontal bands of green, blue, and red colors. Though no traces of floral and leaf designs were found, it seems reasonable to believe that such paintings also existed, comparable to those found at el-Bared, and at the temple of Allat by Ain Shellaleh in the Wadi Ramm.

The deity worshipped at Sela was evidently the same Dushara who is met with so frequently at Petra. Numerous Dushara niches can be seen at Sela. On the southeast side of the top of the hill there stands out prominently a somewhat rounded and almost isolated outspur, in which

Fig. 98. Sela, looking northwest.

(Courtesy Peake Pasha).

Fig. 99.   Nabataean house at Sela.
(Courtesy Peake Pasha).

originally there may have been a small natural cave. This was considerably enlarged by the Nabataeans, who also carved out of the rock inside the cave a large stone pedestal, attached only at the back end to the rear wall of the cave (Fig. 100). This may be considered to be the Dushara throne. The large entrance to the cave faces east, so that the sun in the morning shines full on the Dushara seat. We are reminded of the sacred cave on Mt. Horeb, in which the deity was resident, and at whose entrance Elijah stood with covered countenance hearkening to the word of the Lord.[1]

Fig. 100. Dushara cave and throne at Nabataean Sela.

A place somewhat similar to Sela in its location and arrangements for the conservation of water, is Sheikh er-Rish, which is about 5 kilometers south-southwest of Dana. It is even more unapproachable and difficult of access than Sela. A steep and narrow path, which in many places is little more than a goat track, leads to the foot of the split and turreted chain of hills among which the hill of Sheikh er-Rish stands like a great mountain fortress (Fig. 101). Beside the steep, narrow *siq* which leads to the top of the hill are five large burial (?) chambers. On top of the hill are hillocks, pitted with (Dushara?) niches (Fig. 102). An idea of the nature of these

[1] I Kings 19, 8. 9. 13.

Fig. 101.   Sheikh er-Rish in center, looking south-southwest.

Fig. 102.   Dushara (?) niches on side of hillock, on top of
Sheikh er-Rish.

Fig. 103.   Hillocks of Sheikh Suqut below Sheikh er-Rish.

hillocks can be gained from Fig. 103 which shows the ones called collectively Sheikh Suqut, immediately below Sheikh er-Rish to the northwest, and the countryside beyond it. At Sheikh er-Rish, many of these hillocks were utilized, strange as it may seem, for the purpose of catching and storing water. If there was a reasonably flat area on one of them, a cistern would be sunk into it, with channels cut into the rock to lead the water to it. One of these cisterns was about 2 meters in diameter, and about 3.5 meters deep. Although it was June 23, 1937 when we visited Sheikh er-Rish, long after the spring rains, one of these cisterns still contained a considerable amount of water. Sheikh er-Rish was used in all probability from Nabataean through Byzantine times.

Where springs were available, the Nabataeans would frequently lead water for long distances through aqueducts to irrigate lands which would otherwise have lain fallow. At a Nabataean place called Khirbet Ayun Ghuzlan, within view of the Nabataean temple of Khirbet Tannur, which we shall discuss in more detail below, we found parts of an aqueduct that had been used in an extensive irrigation system. There were numerous, finely hewn blocks of stone with channels cut in them, which were lying about below the springs (Fig. 104). They had only recently been dug up, and obviously many other parts of this aqueduct, which led the water from the springs to the terraced fields descending the hillside below them, are still buried. The amazing ingenuity and skilful resourcefulness of the ancients in Transjordan, shown especially by the Nabataeans and to a high degree also by their successors in the Roman and Byzantine periods, made life possible in the most inhospitable areas. Witness the great Byzantine dams, e. g. the one at Qurnub in southernmost Palestine, which may well have been preceded by similar Nabataean-Roman dams (Fig. 105). The pressure of large, dynamic populations was so great in these periods, that thousands were forced to seek sustenance and shelter in marginal or even waste lands, where normally few might care to or could find a livelihood.

II

Within the last few years the archaeological survey expeditions of the American School of Oriental Research at Jerusalem have examined in the territories in southern Transjordan once occupied by Edom and Moab more than five hundred Nabataean watch-towers, fortresses, villages, and cities, most of them situated in their day in the midst of cultivated fields. These sites can be recognized as Nabataean, even in places where there are no standing ruins, by the evidence of Nabataean pottery. Made of finely

Fig. 104.   Stones from conduit at Khirbet Ayun Ghuzlan.

Fig. 105.   Dam at Qurnub.

levigated clay, which ranged in color from reddish-brown to red to drab between layers of reddish-brown or red, most of these Nabataean potsherds formed parts of unbelievably thin, fragile cups, saucers, shallow dishes, jugs, and bowls of various sizes, and of the most delicate workmanship.

The painted designs on some of this pottery seem to have no traceable affinities with any other pottery. Some of the forms resemble faience pots from Nippur in the University of Pennsylvania Museum, and in fabric are as fine as the thin, yellow, unglazed Achaemenid pottery found at Ur. The painted designs consist usually of stylized floral or leaf patterns in solid reddish-brown color, superimposed over very delicate parallel lines, which may be the stylized representation of the veining of leaves. Other patterns of solid colors may actually represent leaves. Sometimes, however, leaf and floral designs are most faithfully depicted (Fig. 106). The palm leaf design is a very common one. Some sherds of fine ribbed ware were found, while on others were bands of rouletting, the sharp little indentations fitting into each other like rows of diminutive cogwheels (Fig. 107). Some of the pottery was simply wet smoothed.

Whoever has handled Nabataean pottery could never possibly forget it again. Indeed, so clear is the evidence of Nabataean occupation in southern Transjordan furnished by Nabataean pottery, that the northern limit of Nabataean Transjordan may be fixed by the sudden and complete cessation of Nabataean pottery on an east-west line which may be drawn approximately from the north end of the Dead Sea through Madeba to the desert. It is amazing that north of this approximate line no Nabataean pottery is found, except in a few isolated places. This can be understood, we believe, only through the realization that the northern part of the Nabataean kingdom in Syria was reached not through northern Transjordan, but through the Wadi Sirhan. Contemporary pottery in northern Transjordan was of the same late Hellenistic-Roman type characteristic of Palestine. Nabataean pottery has been found in southern Palestine along the Nabataean trade-route leading from the Arabah past Qurnub to Gaza. The Hellenistic and Parthian influences reflected in Nabataean wares and architecture probably came via Syria along the trade-route leading to Arabia through the Wadi Sirhan. Nabataean caravans also travelled through Sinai, and brought back with them influences from Alexandria.

The Nabataean occupation of Edom and Moab was sustained then not only by trade, but to a large degree by widespread and intensive agriculture. In the 4th century B. C., as we learn from Diodorus, the Nabataeans were nomadic Arabs, who, although they already then trafficked in the rich products of Arabia, did not engage in agriculture, lived in tents and not

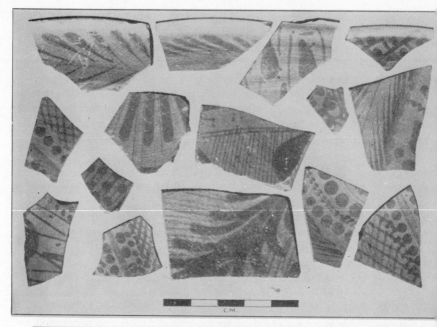

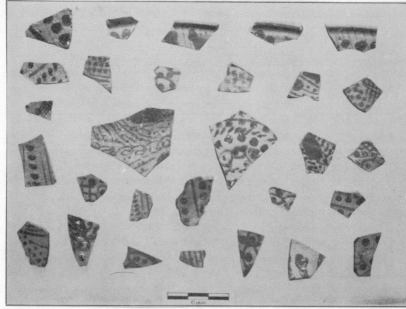

Fig. 106. Painted Nabataean pottery.

Fig. 107. Lined and rouletted Nabataean pottery.

Fig. 108. Nabataean floral ornamentation, from Khirbet Brak near Petra.

houses, and abhorred the use of wine. By the turn of the era, however, Strabo was able correctly to describe the Nabataeans as living in stone houses, being devoted to trade, and engaging in agriculture in a large part of their fertile country. The ban on wine seems definitely to have been overcome. The grape-and-vine-and-leaf motif became one of the most common employed in architectural and ceramic decoration (Fig. 108). The religion was a fertility religion. It is only from the agricultural background of the Nabataean civilization, which flowered between the first centuries B. C. and A. D., that we can properly understand the emerging details of the fertility cults, which they adopted from their surroundings.

III

The most commonly known Nabataean deity is dhu-Shara (Dushara, Dusares, = Dionysus), who was worshipped through the length and breadth of the Nabataean kingdom. Numerous dedications to him in Nabataean and Greek have been found. He was worshipped at Petra, for instance, in the form of an unhewn, four-cornered black stone. The day is past, however, when practically only the lone Dushara stone was known as representing a Nabataean deity. Numerous Nabataean temples have now been discovered in Transjordan, and in them numerous Nabataean gods, whose existence had hitherto not been known. Particularly have they been found in a Nabataean temple called Khirbet Tannur, situated in Transjordan, and excavated by the American School in conjunction with the Transjordan Department of Antiquities.[2]

If one follows the new road which leads from Tafileh northward down to the Wadi Hesa, one comes, a few kilometers before actually reaching the *wadi*, to the el-Aban police-station on the east side of the road. About half an hour's walk west of the police-station, on top of a high, isolated hill called Jebel Tannur, rising steeply at the confluence of the Wadi Hesa and the Wadi el-Aban (La'abani), is Khirbet Tannur (Fig. 109).

The general impression made by the nature of the ruins and the position of the fallen stones at Khirbet Tannur is that the temple there was destroyed by an earthquake. The site was never again occupied, except by some later insignificant squatters. Those sculptured pieces which escaped more or less intact through subsequent centuries, by reason of being partly or completely buried, owe their preservation in large part to the good fortune, which, on the whole, kept the site free from post-Nabataean occupation. The com-

---

[2] The American School's share of the antiquities found is now at the Cincinnati Art Museum.

parative inaccessibility, which impelled the Nabataeans to choose the high Jebel Tannur for their temple, made it unattractive for those who came after them. Such vandalism as has taken place is to be attributed to the benighted fanaticism of the occasional shepherds or goatherds who lead their flocks even to such out of the way places. The excavations revealed the plan of a fairly complete Nabataean temple-complex. A whole pantheon of hitherto unknown Nabataean deities was found in the sanctuary that had become their grave.

The remarkable location of Khirbet Tannur on top of the high Jebel

Fig. 109.   Jebel Tannur.

Tannur is approachable only by a single steep path that twists its way up a ridge on its southeast side. In places the ancient banking of this path is still clearly visible. Near the top it is cut through solid rock. It is quite likely that originally at least the upper and steeper part of the ascent was negotiated by a staircase. It is furthermore not unlikely that the ascent was made in solemn ceremonial procession by parties of pilgrims on sacred occasions.

It seems, indeed, that once having gained the summit, it was as natural to grace the hilltop with a temple as it was for the ancients to adorn a goddess with a crown. To the west the eye follows the course of the great cleft of the Wadi Hesa in its plunge towards the Dead Sea, and to the east its approach from the desert. The rich, green site of Ainch is situated a few miles away to the east on the north slope of the Wadi Hesa. To the south is visible the ascending course of the Wadi el-Aban. There, but a few kilometers distant from Khirbet Tannur, are the ruins of another beautiful Nabataean temple, Qasr edh-Dherih. The somewhat higher east side of the top of the hill, where only the temple stood, was literally covered with building stones of all kinds: bases, drums, capitals, lintels, cornices, doorjambs, and sculptured stones of many types (Fig. 110). In the ruins numerous Nabataean sherds of all kinds were found, including particularly the fine, egg-shell thin, painted, plain, and rouletted wares, and also pieces of terra sigillata of " Pergamene " type (Fig. 111).

Broad steps lead up to a gateway in the center of the east wall of the outer east court of the temple area. An engaged column and a pilaster on which originally were Nabataean capitals, and in a subsequent period Corinthian capitals, decorate the outer façade of the east wall on each side of the gateway. The large outer east court, which is 15.60 meters square, still retains some of its original paving, particularly on its east and west sides. A shallow channel leading from the northeast corner to the southeast corner disposed of the rain water through apertures cut through the outer east wall. A platform two steps high bounds the court on the north and south sides. Over the platform extended a roofed colonnade, whose roof probably slanted downwards toward the court. On the north side of the court near its east end is the podium of a large altar. It is possible that somewhere in the now unpaved area of the court there was also at one time a sacred pool (Fig. 112).

At the west end of the outer court a flight of four steps leads to a gateway in the center of the east side of the temple proper, which is on a platform. The temple, and the shrine within it, face almost due east. The steps are flanked by two engaged columns, with a pilaster and quarter column at each end of the east wall. There are two pilasters at the south and north corners of the west wall, and two pilasters on each of the other walls between the corner pilasters. On these engaged columns and pilasters, whose Attic bases rest on a strong stylobate, there were originally Nabataean capitals, which were replaced in a subsequent period with Corinthian capitals. The quarter columns had also been added in this later period.

On each side of the gateway, between the engaged column and the pilaster, was a shallow niche, crowned by an architrave, over which was a pediment with a dentilated decoration. The architrave is decorated with two rosettes spaced between three triglyphs (Fig. 113) set between two busts of feminine figures in relief. Over the doorway was set a huge bust of Atargatis (Artemis), represented as goddess of foliage and fruit. On her forehead,

Fig. 110.   Surface ruins at Khirbet Tannur.

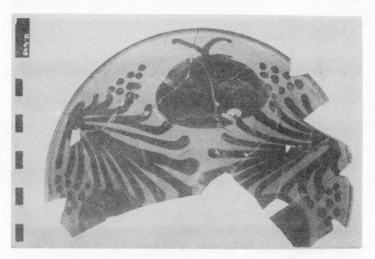

Fig. 111. Partly reconstructed Nabataean bowl from Khirbet Tannur;
decorated with pomegranate, palm-leaf, and date or grape designs,
in reddish brown paint on buff background.

neck, and bosom are leaf decorations, which, however, do not conceal the features (Fig. 114). (A related type of deity of much the same period, in this instance of Zeus, whose features and body are likewise transparently

Fig. 112. Khirbet Tannur. Outer East Court, looking southwest.

Fig. 113. Architrave from Khirbet Tannur.

veiled with large leaves, has been found at Puteoli, north of Naples.) Two side panels, which together with the main centerpiece form a most imposing semi-circular panel, are decorated with vine and leaf and pomegranate and fig motifs. Above the head of the goddess there seems originally to have been a relief of a large eagle and a series of pointed stones set at an angle,

Fig. 114. Atargatis as a goddess of foliage and fruit.

which possibly may be representative of the rays of the sun. The eagle may be identified with Zeus or Zeus-Hadad. The architrave over the columns supported a frieze of busts of representatives of the planets in relief. Six of the seven usually depicted in the religious art of the Hellenistic-Semitic cultural regions were found nearby. There is a Tyche figure in relief on each of the two adjacent sides of the corner stones of this frieze.

In the gateway two door-sills are visible, with sockets in each of them for a separate door, which swung inward. The outer sill was higher than the larger and cruder inner one. It seems that they belonged to two different periods. Near the east end of the south wall of the temple is a small entrance way, through which the proper functionaries entered to open the main east door of the temple, and to attend generally to the needs of the temple.

In the middle of the paved floor of the raised temple-platform stands a small shrine oriented almost exactly due east. During the three building periods of the temple this small shrine was enlarged three times by a new one being built around the preceding one (Fig. 115), much like a series of boxes of various sizes, each larger one enclosing a smaller one. At the corners of the east façade of the shrine are pilasters with quarter columns, and at the corners of the west façade are two square pilasters. A staircase on the south side of the shrine ascends to what must have been a flat top, on which, in all probability, an altar stood. Certainly four, and probably five, of the courses of the pilasters with the quarter columns on the east face of the shrine, consisted of busts in relief of either Atargatis as the " fish-goddess " (Fig. 116) or as the " grain-goddess." Atargatis as the " grain-goddess " is exactly the same in almost all details as the " fish-goddess," except that instead of the fish or dolphins there are ears of grain above and beside her head (Fig. 117). Over the pilasters rested a large architrave, beautifully decorated with a rosette, the egg and dart design, and vine and leaf patterns. This shrine was built around and over an earlier and finer shrine, and it in turn around the earliest and simplest of the three shrines.

Excavation revealed that the top of the second shrine also was reached by a staircase, which in this instance was built along its west side. Two of the steps still remain in position. The upper four courses of the pilasters of the east façade of this smaller and much more daintily built shrine are decorated with rosettes and entwined vine patterns, with the exception that one of the courses in the pilaster on the north end is decorated with a small niche instead of the rosette and vine patterns. In this niche small lamps

Fig. 115. Khirbet Tannur. Inner temple court and shrine, looking west-southwest.

Fig. 116. Atargatis as fish goddess at Khirbet Tannur.

may have been set. Both pilasters, which are set on Attic bases, have caps decorated with the thunderbolt design which was found to be a common motif at Khirbet Tannur. It is visible also at other Nabataean sites. This motif is quite in keeping with the worship of Hadad, one of the chief deities of the Khirbet Tannur temple. Similarly decorated caps were originally on the pilasters on the east façade of the previously mentioned shrine.

Fitting against these pilaster caps of the second shrine, and set over an arch resting on the jambs of the pilasters, was an architrave decorated with a niche and rosettes. Set in the bracket at the spring of the arch are

Fig. 117. Atargatis as grain goddess at Khirbet Tannur.

flint dowels, each of which once held some small figure or other ornamental object. It was in the shallow niche below the arch that there were set, we believe, the magnificent relief of Hadad and another of his consort Atargatis. The present relief of Zeus-Hadad belongs to Period III, the latest period of Khirbet Tannur. Similar or related reliefs may have been there in the preceding period, Period II (Fig. 118)

The figure of the god is sculptured in almost three-quarter relief on a large sandstone block, which is approximately a meter long and 45 centimeters wide (Fig. 119). It is represented as sitting. On a disproportionately small, three-quarter length body, is set a magnificently carved, life-size head. The hair is waved and curled, and the beard and the ends of the flowing moustache are set in snail curls. The top of the head seems to have been crowned with a low *polos* or *kalathos,* which is somewhat damaged. The forehead is low, with two horn-like locks above the center

Fig. 118. East façade of the Shrine of Period II.

Fig. 119.   Zeus-Hadad at Khirbet Tannur.

of the forehead. The shallow-set eyes are shaded by heavy eyebrows; the nose is rather flat; the lips are full, the upper one being somewhat damaged. There are some holes and cracks elsewhere on the face, with one large hole under the right eye. The high girdled *chiton* is fastened by a brooch under the neck. Around the neck is a torque, the ends of which consist of the heads of lions. A similar torque appears around the neck of a small Atargatis figure found nearby. The torques indicate again the multitude of cultural forces, in this particular instance probably Iranian, which influenced the art and architecture of Khirbet Tannur. A fold of the *himation*, partly covering the *chiton*, is thrown over the left shoulder. Beneath the lower end of the fold appears the left hand, with the palm turned inward, grasping the right ear of a young bull,—one of the two bulls which flank the feet of the deity. The middle finger alone is not visible. The raised right arm, which is broken off below the elbow, may originally have held a double-axe or a bundle of wheat. Attached to the fold of the *himation* over the left shoulder and arm is a thunderbolt, extending from the top of the left elbow to the bottom of the hand. The lower arrow head of the thunderbolt is still intact, the upper one having been broken off. The god of the heavens, or the thunder-god Hadad, is frequently represented as adorned with the symbol of the thunderbolt, and as seated between two bulls, one on either side of him.

It seems reasonable to believe that in the same niche, next to the Zeus-Hadad relief, was another relief of the same size consisting of a representation of Atargatis seated between two lions. The basis for this belief is that a small lion's head with part of its body, and a single foot with traces of its mate, were found in the ruins. They are of the same relative size as the bulls beside the seated figure of Zeus-Hadad. Like the Zeus-Hadad relief, they are made of friable sandstone, and there are no other sculptures made of this material. In view also of the important role Atargatis plays in the temple at Khirbet Tannur, and in view of the fact that there is enough room on the east façade of the shrine for two reliefs of the size of the Zeus-Hadad relief to be placed between the front pilasters, it seems quite likely that the sandstone foot and lion are part of a large sandstone relief of Atargatis, which was placed by the side of her consort. Several Zeus-Hadad heads were found at Khirbet Tannur, the rest of the reliefs to which they were originally attached having completely disappeared. One of the heads is approximately of the same type as that of the main Zeus-Hadad (Fig. 120), while another one seems to emphasize Parthian as well as Hellenistic influences (Fig. 121).

In front of the east pilasters of the shrine are two small chambers sunk

Fig. 120.   Zeus-Hadad head from Khirbet Tannur.

Fig. 121.   Hadad head from Khirbet Tannur,
showing Hellenistic-Parthian influences.

into the ground. They were covered with paving blocks, one of them found in position, which could be lifted by inserting one's finger or a hook in a hole in the center of the outside edge of each block. A similar concealed chamber was found in the rear of the shrine. They were evidently offering receptacles, for their contents proved to consist of ashes, charred animal bones, and grains of wheat.

On top of the shrine of the third and latest period there was originally an altar, many of the pieces of which have been recovered, with a tiny feminine head ornamenting the top center of each of its four corner pilasters. Another altar, with a thunderbolt motif on it, was found in position outside the west wall of the inner temple area. It faced an area on the west side of the site which has not yet been excavated. It is noteworthy that the floor of the inner temple area is higher than the floors outside of it. The paved areas on the north and south sides of the inner temple area are, however, on practically the same level as the colonnaded platforms on the north and south sides of the outer east court. The floor of the inner temple court slopes slightly to the east. It is our present belief that this inner temple area with its central shrine was not roofed over, being thus, as also the outer east court with its imposing east façade, built after the fashion of the Egyptian pylon, with the rear or side walls lower and plainer.

We should like to describe briefly here a few of the other numerous sculptures found at Khirbet Tannur. One of the most interesting is a circular panel, with a relief of Tyche in the center (Fig. 122). On her head is a mural crown, which is covered with a hood. The crown, suggesting the turreted walls of an ancient city, indicates clearly the aspect of Tyche as the guardian goddess of the place, a role in which she frequently appears. On the right of her head is the crescent moon, and on the left side a scepter-like symbol. which may possibly be a degenerate representation of a distaff or a quiver. It is composed of a torch bound together with a wand, on the end of which is a broken, crescent moon (?). Encircling this central relief is an outer panel containing the figures of the cycle of the zodiac. Reading counterclockwise to the left from the top center of the zodiac, we see (1) Aries, represented by a Minerva(?) figure, (2) Taurus, (3) Gemini, (4) Cancer, (5) Leo, (6) part of the head of Virgo, and the top of a wand or sheaf she was carrying. Reading clockwise to the right from the top we see (7) Libra, (8) Scorpio, (9) Sagittarius, (10) Capricornus, represented by a Pan(?) figure, and (11) Aquarius, with his bucket upside down. The next panel, which must represent (12) Pisces is completely broken off. The significance of the counter-clockwise and clockwise halves of the zodiac seems to be that there was a natural New Year which began with spring, and a civil New Year which began with autumn.

An unusual type of goddess found at Khirbet Tannur is the winged Tyche-Nike holding aloft a horn of plenty, combining the characteristics of Tyche, the goddess of fortune, with those of Nike, the goddess of victory. Heads of related Nike figures were found invariably broken off of the bodies

Fig. 122. Relief of Tyche, surrounded by a zodiac panel, from Khirbet Tannur.

to which they belonged, whether as the result of malice or accident it being impossible to determine. The Nike reliefs, and others like them, evidently belonged to friezes ornamenting the walls of the inner temple. An almost intact incense altar was found (Fig. 123), with a central panel containing a relief of Zeus-Hadad, and two side panels with reliefs of winged Nikes. The altar was inscribed with a Greek dedicatory inscription, part of which unfortunately has been broken off. It reads: " (ALEX) ANDROS AMROU," combining thus a Greek forename with a Nabataean family name. Several other fragments of Greek inscriptions were found, and two Nabataean inscriptions. A pillar-drum was found with the same Nike figures in relief on it as on the incense altar. A fine relief of Helios was found, among other representations of the planets.

The deities of the Nabataean temple at Khirbet Tannur were primarily the deities of Syria. They call to mind the gods of Hierapolis-Bambyke, of Heliopolis-Baalbek, of Palmyra, of Dura-Europos, and also of Ascalon,

Fig. 123. Left). Front panel of incense altar, showing Zeus-Hadad with staff in right hand, and indistinct thunder-bolt over lower part of left arm. Right). Left side panel of incense altar, with relief of winged Tyche holding a palm branch in the left hand and a wreath in the outstretched right hand.

among other places. Particularly do the figures of Atargatis and Zeus-Hadad at Khirbet Tannur remind one vividly of the bas-relief of Atargatis and Hadad found in the ruins of the temple of Atargatis at Dura. One is also reminded of the fact that the Nabataean trade-route leading to Gaza served to bring the Nabataeans into contact with the "fish-goddess" Atargatis of Ascalon. The entire ruined temple at Khirbet Tannur, with its beautiful friezes and its representations of deities, presents a mixture of

Hellenistic, Syrian, Egyptian, and Parthian influences, which was characteristic of the eclectic nature of the Nabataean civilization.

These deities were worshipped at a number of other Nabataean temples in southern Transjordan, such as Mesheirfeh, Kerak, Khirbet Dherih, Dhat Ras, Aineh, Qasr Rabbah, Petra and Ramm. Helios busts in relief have been found at Mesheirfeh, Kerak, and Qasr Rabbah (Fig. 124). At Qasr Rabbah, there are also sculptured heads of lions, a beautiful gazelle (Fig. 125), a panther, a winged Eros, a ram's head, among others, all of which we consider to belong to the same time as the last period at Khirbet Tannur; i. e., to about the first quarter of the 2nd century A. D. It is to the last or third period at Khirbet Tannur that we assign, for instance, the representations of Atargatis as the " fish " or " grain " goddess, and all the other sculptures found there. To this period also belong the sculptures visible at Khirbet edh-Dherih. Qasr Rabbah, if work there is properly financed, will yield, we believe, very rich results for those interested in adding to our growing knowledge of Nabataean civilization. The temple and gods of Khirbet Tannur are, it is clear, not unique in southern Transjordan (Fig. 126).

IV

What the first Nabataean caravans may have seen on Jebel Tannur, as they traversed the " King's Highway " and made one of their halts by Jebel Tannur, is a matter of pure conjecture. The site may have enjoyed a pre-Nabataean sanctity, possessing perhaps a sacred dolmen or even a counterpart of the Baluah stele. We believe that some time early in the first century B. C. a temple with an inner shrine was constructed at Khirbet Tannur, probably replacing a simple altar. To judge from the debris of grain offerings and small animal sacrifices from the two later shrines, one may assume that similar offerings were brought during the period of the first shrine, which we shall hereafter designate as " Shrine I." It was much used and carefully preserved. When one of the stone blocks in the bottom course of its north wall somehow or other got broken, the remaining parts were carefully reinforced with thick lime plaster. Indeed one of the main characteristics of the entire temple-complex in general, and of the smaller inner shrine in particular, was the great respect entertained in each period of reconstruction or enlargement for the remains of the preceding period. Shrine I was probably the central point of the temple-area, whose rough rubble walls were partly re-used in later periods.

A considerable period after the contruction of shrine I, and some time before the construction of shrine II, perhaps in the third quarter of the first

Fig. 124.   Helios relief from Qasr Rabbah.
(Photographed for the American School by courtesy
of the Palestine Archaeological Museum).

Fig. 125.   Gazelle from Qasr Rabbah.
(Photographed for the American School by courtesy
of the Palestine Archaeological Museum).

14

century B. C., the shrine had apparently so grown in importance and popu-
larity and wealth, corresponding to the rapid development of the Nabataean
kingdom as a whole, that a well made, dressed-stone pavement was laid in
the raised inner temple-area around shrine I. The laying of the pavement
around the simple box-like shrine (or altar basis) may be compared to the
construction of the Dome of the Rock around the Holy Rock at Jerusalem,
whose sanctity probably goes back to early antiquity. A better example,
perhaps, may be the Meccan Ka'ba, which is built of layers of gray stone,

Fig. 126. Lion's head from Khirbet Tannur. A similar head found there
was used as a water spout.

with the black stone built into the wall at its eastern corner, and with an
open paved courtyard built around it. Indeed, the inner box-like shrine of
Khirbet Tannur, which as we have seen, in each succeeding period was
simply encased in a larger box, may hark back for the idea of its origin to
the sacred betyls familiar to the Nabataeans from Arabia, the land of their
origin.

Up to approximately the third quarter of the first century B. C., shrine I,
with the subsequently built pavement around it, continued in use. Then
it became necessary either to rebuilt shrine I, which may have been damaged
by an earthquake to the extent of its front side being destroyed and its
north side leaning dangerously outward (not to speak of the other two

sides, which cannot be examined at present), or to build a completely new shrine around and over it. The latter was actually done. None of the building stones of shrine I were re-used, nor was any part of its remaining walls tampered with in any way, partly, we believe, because of the reverence in which it was held, and partly because it was used architecturally as the core of the new structure.

It is impossible to say exactly when the pavement placed against shrine I was laid, but we can say that there is a close relationship between it and shrine II. The masonry work on the pavement blocks, and the general size of the blocks, are completely unlike the workmanship and materials in shrine I, but closely related to those in shrine II. Indeed, before the concluding period of excavations, we had every reason to believe that the pavement was contemporary with shrine II. It was only when the north wall of shrine II was removed that it became apparent that the pavement went under this wall up to the plinth of shrine I. It seems altogether impossible that the builders of shrine II first laid the pavement and then put the walls of their shrine over it. Had they not already had the pavement, they would most probably have sunk the walls of their comparatively heavy shrine considerably below the pavement level. As it was, the paving blocks under the pilaster bases of the east and west corners of the north side of shrine II were depressed below their proper level by reason of the weight above them.

To the period of the second shrine and the fairly elaborate temple-complex built up around it belongs, we believe, a Nabataean inscription dated 7 B. C., discovered beside it. This dedicatory inscription on a stone block of the general type used in shrine and temple II was imbedded originally in a wall. There is the possibility that it commemorated the building of shrine II itself, although exactly which building or monument it commemorated is not known. The much worn inscription, as deciphered with considerable difficulty by Père R. Savignac, director of the École Biblique et Archéologique Française, Jerusalem, reads:

1. (The monument) built by Naṭayr'el the son of
2. Zayda to R'S'YN L'BN for the life of Ḥaretat
3. king of the Nabataeans who loves his people, and for the life of Huldû
4. his wife in the year II.

While some of the letters may be debatable, the dedication to Haretat and Huldu in the year 2 is unquestionable. Haretat, whose wife was Huldu, was Aretas IV, who ruled from 9 B. C. to 40 A. D. The second year of his reign yields the date 7 B. C.

The third shrine can be dated by its architecture, sculpture, and pottery to about the first quarter of the 2nd century A. D. Like its predecessors, it was oriented almost exactly due east, and was destroyed by an earthquake. On the basis of the excavation finds we would now date the history of Khirbet Tannur from about 25 B. C. to 125 A. D. It is important to note that the fine, painted, egg-shell thin Nabataean sherds found at Khirbet Tannur definitely predominate in the earlier levels.

There is a series of rooms on the north and south sides of the inner temple area and the outer court, where, in all probability, the temple functionaries lived and the pilgrims feasted and lodged. These rooms were well paved, with a high bench-like platform going around three sides of each room. The roofs of these chambers (triclinia) were supported by square pillars, whose courses are composed of three triangular stones. The triclinia are important for a number of reasons. They furnish us with knowledge concerning the ritual observed at Khirbet Tannur, according to which feasting (probably after sacrificing and partly of the sacrifices) must have played a very prominent role. They are directly related to the triclinia commonly found in Petra, and indicate the closest relationship between the rituals of Petra and Khirbet Tannur. The only difference between the triclinia of these two places is that at Petra the benches were cut out of soft sandstone, while at Khirbet Tannur they were constructed of well dressed and coursed building blocks. It seems likely that triclinia will be found at other Nabataean sites.

The general adoption of triclinia by the Nabataeans, coupled with the common occurrence of triclinia in Syria, in such places as Antioch, Dura-Europos, and Khirbet Semrin (and also in the temple of the Syrian gods at Delos, dated to the second half of the 2nd century B. C.), points to the widely prevailing practice of the celebration of the cult-meal in the ancient Near East during the first centuries B. C. and A. D. We feel that extensive excavations at Petra will reveal additional similarities between it and Khirbet Tannur, particularly in the form of sculptures of gods and goddesses. The recent discovery at Petra of a plaster model of an excellently fashioned head indicates probably the presence of many other sculptures there. It is difficult to believe that the pantheon of gods discovered at Khirbet Tannur should be so completely missing from Petra, where at present we know only of the Dushara-niches. The Dushara-niches do not occur at Khirbet Tannur.

In addition to pointing out the connection between the triclinia of Khirbet Tannur with those of Petra, one may point out the striking resemblance of the temple plan of Khirbet Tannur, with its outer east court, low platform on north and south sides, and steps rising to a raised inner level, supporting

a shrine on which an altar rested, to the Great High Place of Zibb Atuf at
Petra (Fig. 127). This is (1) built on a mountain top; (2) its outer east
court, which is a large triclinium, is sloped to drain off the rain water:
(3) it is oriented east; (4) there is an altar-base in the outer east court:
(5) steps lead up to a raised altar-block. It seems to us that these similarities are too striking to be accidental, and that the general plan conforms
to a significant arrangement which was purposed, and will in all probability
be found to be wide-spread. It is interesting in this connection to read the
description of the temple at Hierapolis in Lucian's *De Dea Syria*:

Fig. 127.   Great high-place at Petra.

(Courtesy Palestine Department of Antiquities).

As for the temple, it looks to the rising sun. In appearance and in workmanship,
it is like the temples which they build in Ionia; the foundation rises from the
earth to the space of two fathoms, and on this rests the temple. The ascent to the
temple is built of wood and not particularly wide; as you mount, even the great
hall exhibits a wonderful spectacle and it is ornamented with golden doors. . . .
But the temple within is not uniform. *A special sacred shrine is reared within it;*
the ascent to this likewise is not steep [italics are mine], nor is it fitted with doors,
but is entirely open as you approach it. The great temple is open to all; the sacred
shrine to the priests alone and not to all even of these, but only to those who are
deemed nearest to the gods, and who have charge of the entire administration of
the sacred rites. In this shrine are placed the statues, one of which is Hera, the
other Zeus, though they call him by another name. Both of these are golden; both
are sitting; Hera is supported by lions, Zeus is sitting on bulls. . . .

These are some of the numerous indications of the close relationship
between the civilization of the Nabataeans and that of their contemporaries

in the ancient Near East. This applies particularly to the period between the first two centuries B. C. and the first two centuries A. D. Literary language, religion, architecture, and art were more or less the same in places as far apart as Khirbet Tannur in southern Transjordan and Si' in southern Syria. Petra and Baalbek, despite their pronounced differences, had far more in common with each other than might be imagined at first comparison. The weary miles stretching between Antioch on the Orontes, Aila on the eastern arm of the Red Sea, and Ascalon on the Mediterranean, seem to be in inverse ratio to the general community of culture in which all of them were contained.

In general the Nabataeans may be accounted one of the most remarkable peoples that have ever crossed the stage of history. Sprung swiftly out of the deserts of Arabia to a position of great power and affluence and glory, they were thrust back by the Romans even more swiftly into the limbo of history whence they came. While their turn lasted, the Nabataeans wrought greatly, developing overnight, almost, into builders of magnificent cities, unique in the history of the handiwork of man. They were tradesmen, and farmers, and engineers, and architects of great energy and skill. The ruins which they left behind them testify eloquently to the glory which was theirs.

INDEX

201

Date Due

OC 31 '63			
OC 2 '67			
OCT 1 0 '68			
MAY 1 2 '70			
APR 21 '71			
NO 07			
PRINTED	IN U. S. A.		

Library